101

PEOPLE

of the BIBLE

You Should Know

P9-EMR-127

Writing and compilation by Christopher D. Hudson with
David Barrett and Benjamin D. Irwin, of Hudson & Associates.

101

PEOPLE

of the BIBLE

You Should Know

{ Famous, Not-So-Famous, Sometimes Infamous }

BARBOUR
PUBLISHING

ISBN 978-1-61626-361-4

Published by Barbour Publishing, Inc., P.O. Box 719, Uhrichsville, Ohio 44683, www.barbourbooks.com

Our mission is to publish and distribute inspirational products offering exceptional value and biblical encouragement to the masses.

Member of the
Evangelical Christian
Publishers Association

Printed in the Unites States of America.

CONTENTS

INTRODUCTION

Therefore, since we are surrounded by so great a cloud of witnesses,
let us also lay aside every weight and the sin that clings so closely,
and let us run with perseverance the race that is set before us.
HEBREWS 12:1 NRSV

Bible studies and Sunday school classes can fill our minds with many important facts. Through them we learn names of cities, recount historical events, and memorize favorite verses. And though every bit of Bible knowledge we learn can be worthwhile, sometimes we forget one of the most basic characteristics of the Bible: that it's a book about people.

Though these men and women lived thousands of years before us, we share a similar human journey. Together we enjoy the pleasures of life and learn to look to God when faced with devastating pain. Along with them, we experience the excitement of young love, the challenges of raising a family, and the complexities of trying to live for God in a fallen world.

Though we're separated by the years, we're joined by a common human spirit, and we serve a God who spans the ages. As we live in our modern communities, we have the opportunity to learn from those who have gone before us—both from the good and the bad.

We pray that as you read the stories of these lives, you will find your own life changed as well.

ꓯꓯRoN

BROTHER OF MOSES

Now if perfection was through the Levitical priesthood (for on the basis of it the people received the Law), what further need was there for another priest to arise according to the order of Melchizedek, and not be designated according to the order of Aaron?
HEBREWS 7:11 NASB

Ordinary leaders often become remarkable leaders because of extraordinary support. While Moses was arguably the greatest Hebrew leader during Bible times, much of his success came with the help of his brother, Aaron. Aaron stood alongside Moses as they confronted Pharaoh, and he compensated for Moses' weakness by often serving as Moses' spokesperson (see Exodus 4:10). And though Moses served as the principal leader of the Hebrew people, Aaron also held an important position of influence.

It was Aaron's staff that became a snake before Pharaoh (Exodus 7:10). That same staff also turned Egypt's water into blood (Exodus 7:19), brought frogs on the Egyptians (Exodus 8:5), and caused gnats to swarm the Egyptians (Exodus 8:16). Aaron and his sons became the first Hebrew priests appointed by God (Exodus 28:3). The significance of their role as intermediaries between God and the Hebrews became clearly evidenced when they interceded for the people after the rebellion of Korah, Dathan, and Abiram (Numbers 16).

While Aaron usually provided loyal assistance to Moses,

he also experienced some notable failures as a supporter. For example, Aaron and his sister, Miriam, received a sound reprimand from God when they spoke against Moses for marrying a Cushite (Numbers 12:1–15). On another occasion, Aaron buckled under the pressure of the people and created a golden calf while Moses communed with God away from the camp (Exodus 32). As the people approached the Promised Land, Aaron died at the age of 123 on Mount Hor (Numbers 33:39).

Spiritual Insight:

Though generally a good priest, Aaron's imperfection became an important theological symbol. In spite of faithful service to the people of God, Hebrew priests could not provide the perfect intercession required to obtain God's complete forgiveness. Their service illustrated the need for something more, something better. God met that need through the perfect priesthood initiated by Jesus Christ (see Hebrews 5:4; 7:11).

Meaning:
Uncertain

First Reference:
Exodus 4:14

Last Reference:
Hebrews 9:4

Key References:
Exodus 4:30; 32:2–4; Leviticus 9:7

ABIGAIL

NABAL'S WIDOW AND DAVID'S WIFE

*David said to Abigail, "Praise be to the LORD, the God of Israel,
who has sent you today to meet me. May you be blessed for your good
judgment and for keeping me from bloodshed this day and from
avenging myself with my own hands."*
1 SAMUEL 25:32–33 NIV

Everyone has needed an Abigail at some point in life—someone who, through discretion and grace, has kept us from doing something we would really regret.

Abigail was the wife of a wealthy herder named Nabal, whose name means "fool." While David was on the run from Saul, he spent some time in the area near Nabal's flocks and kept them safe from potential thieves. When the time came for Nabal's sheep to be sheared, David sent his men to receive some payment for their services, but Nabal rebuffed them and sent them away empty-handed. When David heard about this, he was furious and gathered his men to go kill every one of Nabal's men.

But Abigail, whom the Bible describes as discerning and beautiful, intercepted David before he reached Nabal's men, offered him some food, and persuaded him to turn back from repaying Nabal for his affront.

David immediately recognized the wisdom in Abigail's words, turned back from his vengeance, and praised God for using Abigail to save him from doing something he would have regretted (1 Samuel 25).

When Abigail informed her husband of all that transpired between her and David, Nabal's "heart failed him and he became like a stone" (1 Samuel 25:37 NIV). Ten days later Nabal died, and David took Abigail as his wife.

Related Information:

David once had to rescue Abigail and one of his other wives from the Amalekites, who had raided his town of Ziklag and carried off many people (1 Samuel 30).

Meaning:
Source of joy

First Reference:
1 Samuel 25:3

Last Reference:
1 Chronicles 3:1

ABRAHAM

PATRIARCH OF ISRAEL

The LORD had said to Abram [Abraham], "Go from your country, your
people and your father's household to the land I will show you.
I will make you into a great nation, and I will bless you; I will make
your name great, and you will be a blessing."
GENESIS 12:1–2 NIV

Abraham is a paragon of faith. He lived in a world that
regarded family and tribe as security, but the Lord called
him to leave his family, people, and country and travel to a different land—and Abraham did so without question! The land
that the Lord was going to give Abraham's descendants was
already well settled, so how could he "inherit" this land? Finally,
his wife was in her sixties—well past childbearing years—so
how could he ever expect to have any descendants at all
(Genesis 12)?

But Abraham trusted God and His promises, and his faith
was rewarded. Abraham and Sarah eventually bore Isaac, who
fathered Jacob, who fathered the leaders of the twelve tribes of
Israel. Many years later, the Israelites conquered the Promised
Land of Canaan and occupied it as their inheritance. God was
indeed faithful.

Abraham was not without his times of doubt. For instance,
on two separate occasions he lied about his wife in order to protect his life (Genesis 12, 20). Abraham also expressed doubt that
he would bear a son to carry on his name and estate (Genesis

15:1–3). Nevertheless, when the Lord made promises to Abraham, he "believed the LORD, and he credited it to him as righteousness" (Genesis 15:6 NIV).

Spiritual Insight:

While Abraham is certainly a great example of faith for Christians today, that is not all he is to us. We are also his very children, the descendants whom God had promised to give him and to bless. Paul makes this clear in his letter to the Galatians: "Understand, then, that those who have faith are children of Abraham" (Galatians 3:7 NIV). Thank God that all His faithful promises are made available even to us who believe Him today.

Meaning:
Father of a multitude

First Reference:
Genesis 17:5

Last Reference:
1 Peter 3:6

Key References:
Genesis 17:2–8; 22:8

Ahab

KING OF ISRAEL

And Ahab the son of Omri did evil in the sight of the LORD,
more than all who were before him.
1 KINGS 16:30 ESV

As Ahab's life shows, God's favor often has little to do with worldly success. By all worldly accounts, Ahab was a very successful leader. He ruled as king over Israel for twenty-two years (1 Kings 16:29), cementing his power through a shrewd political marriage to Jezebel, daughter of the king of Tyre. He was successful in several military campaigns and even persuaded the king of Judah to join him in his attempt to recover the city of Ramoth Gilead from the Arameans (1 Kings 22:3–4). Assyrian records recall how Ahab spearheaded a coalition of forces to fight against the Assyrians at Qarqar, and his own contribution of over half the chariots for the coalition demonstrates his great military strength in comparison to neighboring nations.

So does Ahab's great success reveal that God was pleased with him? Not at all. The Bible makes it clear that Ahab sinned more than all the kings of Israel before him (1 Kings 16:30), and God was greatly displeased with him. Ahab's marriage to Jezebel led him and his people to worship Baal and other idols, and his reign was marked by wickedness. In the end, the Lord ordained that Ahab would be killed by an archer as Israel fought against the Arameans to recover Ramoth Gilead, and his wife, Jezebel, would suffer a shameful death as well (2 Kings 9:30–37).

Spiritual Insight:

First Samuel 16:7 makes it clear that "the LORD sees not as man sees: man looks on the outward appearance, but the LORD looks on the heart" (1 Samuel 16:7 ESV). It may have appeared to everyone else that Ahab was successful and enjoyed God's favor, but his heart was sold to wickedness, and God was not pleased with him. God is pleased when we humbly seek Him and turn from our wickedness, calling on Him to forgive us and change us to reflect His character (Micah 6:8; Romans 12:1).

Meaning:
Friend of his father

First Reference:
1 Kings 16:28

Last Reference:
Micah 6:16

Key Reference:
1 Kings 16:29–30

ANNA

PROPHETESS AND WIDOW WHO LIVED IN THE TEMPLE

*There was also a prophet, Anna. . . . She was very old; she had lived
with her husband seven years after her marriage, and then was
a widow until she was eighty-four. She never left the temple but
worshiped night and day, fasting and praying.*
LUKE 2:36–37 NIV

It's almost too hard to imagine what that moment must have
been like for Anna. For probably sixty years she had been a
widow living at the temple, worshipping night and day, fasting
and praying, even communicating prophecies to people. No
doubt many of her thoughts and prayers focused on the coming Messiah and the redemption of Jerusalem.

Then all of a sudden, there He was—the Messiah—right
in front of her. She heard what godly Simeon had said about
Him, about how this baby was the Lord's salvation and a light
to the Gentiles. Could it really be true?

Anna came up to Mary and Joseph, thanking God for them
and for their little baby, Jesus, the Savior of the world. What else
could she say to them except thanks to God? Anna had plenty to
say later, though—to everyone she met who was looking forward
to the redemption of Jerusalem. She told them all about the baby
she had seen in the temple and the hope that He was bringing
to the entire world. Anna had seen the Messiah.

Related Information:

Most scholars place Jesus' birth at about 5 BC, which means that Anna would have been about twenty-six years old (and perhaps recently widowed) when the independent kingdom of Israel under the Hasmoneans was overtaken by the vast Roman Empire. Perhaps this is what led her to commit herself to fasting and praying day and night in the temple for the rest of her life.

Meaning:
Favored

Only Reference:
Luke 2:36

Aquila and Priscilla

PROMINENT IN THE EARLY CHURCH

There [in Corinth] he [Paul] met a Jew named Aquila, a native of Pontus, who had recently come from Italy with his wife Priscilla, because Claudius had ordered all Jews to leave Rome. Paul went to see them, and because he was a tentmaker as they were, he stayed and worked with them.

ACTS 18:2–3 NIV

Aquila and his wife, Priscilla, were truly coworkers of Paul in the fullest sense of the word. Paul refers to them as his "fellow workers" in Romans 16:3 NASB, meaning they shared in his work of spreading the gospel among the Gentiles. Yet they were even his coworkers in the secular sense of being fellow tent makers (Acts 18:3).

Aquila was originally from Pontus, a region on the southeast coast of the Black Sea, but at some point he and his wife moved to Rome. Eventually they had to leave Rome, too, because they were Jews, and the emperor expelled all Jews from Rome. That is how they came to be in Corinth when Paul arrived there after delivering his speech to the Areopagus in Athens.

Paul no doubt taught Aquila and his wife the gospel well while they were with him at Corinth, and then they accompanied him to Ephesus (Acts 18:18–19). Paul left them there while he himself went on to Jerusalem and then back to his home church of Antioch. In the meantime, Aquila and Priscilla demonstrated their true understanding of the gospel by helping Apollos, a very skilled, learned Bible teacher in his own right, come to know the gospel more adequately (Acts 18:26).

At some point, the couple must have traveled back to Rome for a time, because Paul greeted them in his letter to the Romans (Romans 16:3). Then they must have returned to Ephesus, because Paul greeted them again in a letter to Timothy, whom Paul had sent to Ephesus (2 Timothy 4:19).

Did You Know?

Corinth and Ephesus were among the busiest, wealthiest cities of the Roman Empire. It is possible that Aquila and Priscilla chose to live and work in these cities because they could find abundant demand for their tent-making skills.

Meaning (Aquila):
Eagle

Meaning (Priscilla):
--

First Reference:
Acts 18:2

First Reference:
Acts 18:2

Last Reference:
2 Timothy 4:19

Last Reference:
1 Corinthians 16:19

Balaam

Prophet with a Talking Donkey

*And the donkey said to Balaam, "Am I not your donkey,
on which you have ridden all your life long to this day?
Is it my habit to treat you this way?"*
Numbers 22:30 esv

The tale of Balaam and his talking donkey fascinates children, but his story carries a greater significance than what may be seen on the surface. When examined more deeply, the biblical narrative regarding Balaam ultimately points to the power and supremacy of God.

Biblical and archaeological history both confirm that Balaam was a renowned seer in the ancient world. When Balaak, king of Moab, felt threatened by the Hebrews, he summoned Balaam. He hoped to hire Balaam to curse the Hebrews.

Even though Balaam was a spiritual person, there is no indication that he was a true prophet of God. He did, however, appear to know of God's power and feared Him enough to turn down Balaak's initial request. When Balaak persisted with offers of financial gain, Balaam agreed to meet him. (Read the entire story in Numbers 22–24.) On Balaam's trek to Moab, God confronted the seer with profound reminders of His power: an angel with a flaming sword and a talking donkey (Numbers 22:27–28). With a stern rebuke and severe warning, God permitted Balaam to proceed on his journey. Arriving at his destination with God's admonition fresh in his mind, Balaam refused to curse the people of God but blessed them three times instead.

Balaam's story illustrates how the power of God trumps the evil intents of others. By using a talking donkey and a sinful seer, God showed that He can use anyone or anything to accomplish His plan—even unwilling or unusual participants.

Spiritual Insight:

Balaam's story includes more than the episode involving a talking donkey. Revelation 2:14 and Numbers 31:16 reveal that Balaam instructed Balaak to lead the Israelites into idolatry and sexual sin. Balaam's story ended when he died in battle against the Israelites as recorded in Numbers 31:8.

Meaning:
Foreigner

First Reference:
Numbers 22:5

Last Reference:
Revelation 2:14

Key References:
Numbers 22:18; 23:12; Revelation 2:14–15

Barabbas

Prisoner with Jesus

So Pilate, wishing to satisfy the crowd, released for them Barabbas,
and having scourged Jesus, he delivered him to be crucified.
Mark 15:15 ESV

To hear it makes our blood boil: A guilty man goes free, and an innocent man is condemned instead. For most of us, this will be the only association we ever have with the name Barabbas.

All we know about Barabbas himself is that he was a notorious prisoner who had been imprisoned for insurrection and murder some time before Jesus' arrest (Matthew 27:16; Mark 15:7; Luke 23:19; John 18:40). We don't know anything about the insurrection, nor do we know what happened to Barabbas after his release.

The only other thing we know about Barabbas is that this guilty man, for no reason other than the will of God carried out by Pontius Pilate, was released and set free, and Jesus, an innocent man, was condemned and executed instead. It all happened as part of Pilate's usual custom of releasing a prisoner chosen by the crowd during Passover (Matthew 27:15; Mark 15:6; John 18:39), and this time the religious leaders succeeded in stirring up the crowd to choose Barabbas instead of Jesus.

Spiritual Insight:

It is completely right to be angry when we hear of such injustice being committed against Jesus, an innocent man. Yet if we reflect on our own salvation, every believer has stood precisely in Barabbas's place. We, being undeniably guilty in our sins, have been released from our death sentence for no reason of our own—it is simply by the gracious will of God—and Jesus has been condemned and executed in our place. From now on, when you hear the name Barabbas, praise God for the immeasurable grace He has shown every believer, and thank Him that you—though undeserving—have been set free to serve Him.

Meaning:
Son of Abba

First Reference:
Matthew 27:16

Last Reference:
John 18:40

Key References:
Matthew 27:17, 21–22

BARNABAS

APOSTLE AND COWORKER OF PAUL

Thus Joseph, who was also called by the apostles Barnabas (which means son of encouragement), a Levite, a native of Cyprus. . .
ACTS 4:36 ESV

If people from your church gave you a nickname, what would it be? The Great Helper? Miss Generous? Captain Gossip? We don't usually give people such overtly suggestive nicknames, but people in Jesus' day did. One such nickname for a leader in the early church was Barnabas, meaning "son of encouragement," and the nickname couldn't have been more fitting.

We first hear of Barnabas, whose given name was Joseph, during the early days of the church. The Bible notes how at that time the believers were of one mind, and no one was needy—because from time to time believers would sell some possessions and bring the money to the leaders for distribution (Acts 4:32–35). Barnabas is mentioned as being one of those generous people.

Later Barnabas is mentioned again as the one who stood up for Paul (also called Saul) before the other apostles in Jerusalem when Paul first became a believer (Acts 9:27). Barnabas also traveled to Tarsus, Paul's hometown, to ask him to join in ministry at Antioch (Acts 11:25). Barnabas went with Paul on their first missionary journey (Acts 13:1–3). At the outset of their second journey, Barnabas was such a believer in people that he could not bear to exclude his relative Mark, who had abandoned them on the first journey, even though Paul was insistent that Mark not be allowed to come (Acts 15:36–41).

Spiritual Insight:

Barnabas's encouraging nature was so apparent to everyone that they nicknamed him Son of Encouragement. Take a moment to consider what your most recognizable traits are. Are you seen as a person who encourages? Who helps? Who gives? Or would others see you as someone who criticizes? Who avoids church work days? Who is tightfisted? Ask God to help you become a person who is characterized by the fruit of the Spirit (Galatians 5:22–23).

Meaning:
Son of encouragement

First Reference:
Acts 4:36

Last Reference:
Colossians 4:10

Key References:
Acts 9:26–27; 11:22–24

Bartimaeus

Blind Beggar Who Saw Jesus

And Jesus said to him, "What do you want me to do for you?" And the blind man said to him, "Rabbi, let me recover my sight." And Jesus said to him, "Go your way; your faith has made you well." And immediately he recovered his sight and followed him on the way.

Mark 10:51–52 ESV

We don't often see miracles happening at the corner coffee shop or outside our local courthouse. But the crowds pressing through the city gates of Jericho certainly witnessed one as Jesus passed through their city one day long ago (Mark 10:46).

By the dusty roadside near the Jericho gate sat Bartimaeus, a blind man, begging from the ground among the jostling crowd. Suddenly, he heard a large crowd moving by and learned that Jesus of Nazareth was among them. Jesus! No more begging, he began shouting, "'Jesus, Son of David, have mercy on me!'" (Mark 10:47 ESV). The people around him reprimanded him for his noise, but he only shouted all the louder for the merciful Son of David.

Jesus must have heard his cry, for He stopped and told the crowd to call Bartimaeus to Him. Quickly casting aside his cloak, Bartimaeus went to meet Jesus and told Him simply, "Rabbi, I want to see." Jesus replied, "Go. . . your faith has healed you'" (Mark 10:51–52 NIV), and a healed, seeing Bartimaeus followed Him away from Jericho.

Spiritual Insight:

Bartimaeus fervently called to Jesus because he recognized who Jesus was: the merciful Son of David. He was excited to be in the presence of the One who mercifully healed and worked in even the most seemingly impossible situations. Heal a blind person? Make him see? Bartimaeus had little doubt. He knew Jesus could heal him. What is our heart's attitude when we approach our Savior during difficult or traumatic times in life? Do we doubt His care, mercy, and ability to work for our good, or do we have the confidence of Bartimaeus when we call out, "Jesus, Son of David, have mercy on me"?

Meaning:
Son of Timaeus

Only Reference:
Mark 10:46

BENJaMiN

BROTHER OF JOSEPH

*As [Joseph] looked about and saw his brother Benjamin, his own
mother's son, he asked, "Is this your youngest brother, the one you told
me about?" And he said, "God be gracious to you, my son."*
GENESIS 43:29 NIV

Some things never change. Brothers can fight among themselves like cats and dogs, but in the end, few other relationships are marked by greater loyalty and love than a brother for
a brother. The relationship between Benjamin and Joseph may
have been no different.

Benjamin was the younger brother of Joseph and the son
of Rachel, the beloved wife of Jacob. Benjamin had eleven
brothers in all, but only Joseph was his full brother. All the others were born to different mothers. Rachel died giving birth to
Benjamin, and she wanted to name him Ben-Oni ("son of my
sorrow"), but Jacob named him Benjamin ("son of my right
hand/strength") instead (Genesis 35:18).

After Joseph had been sold into slavery by his brothers and
had risen to a very high position within the Egyptian government, Joseph's brothers came to Egypt looking for food. They
did not recognize Joseph when they saw him, but he recognized them. Joseph tested his brothers' hearts to see how they
would respond, in the process blessing Benjamin much more
than his brothers and showing his special love for the youngest. Eventually Joseph revealed his identity to the brothers and

convinced them to move to Egypt with him. He continued to richly bless Benjamin with money and clothes (Genesis 45:22).

Related Information:

Benjamin eventually became the father of a tribe of Israel by the same name, and these people were known as able warriors, many of whom were left-handed and able to sling a stone with great accuracy (Judges 20:15–16).

Meaning:
Son of the right hand

First Reference:
Genesis 35:18

Last Reference:
1 Chronicles 8:1

BEZALEL

BUILDER OF THE TABERNACLE

*"Bezalel and Oholiab and every craftsman in whom the LORD
has put skill and intelligence to know how to do any work
in the construction of the sanctuary shall work in accordance
with all that the LORD has commanded."*
EXODUS 36:1 ESV

Given the Bible's strong emphasis on godly living and faithfulness to the Lord, it might be tempting to think that such things as art and architecture are essentially secular, second-class concerns of God. The Lord's commission to Bezalel, however, proves this idea very wrong.

While Moses was on Mount Sinai, the Lord gave him very specific plans regarding how His people were to live and worship. Part of those plans included the construction of the tabernacle, essentially a mobile worship tent that housed the ark of the covenant and the altar. The Lord gave very specific instructions regarding how the tabernacle was to be built and how the priests were to dress and perform their duties. The Lord designated a man named Bezalel to head a team of artists to produce all the objects involved in worship. These people were skilled in working with gold, silver, bronze, stone, wood, and even fabric, and they were to use their skills to glorify God and lead others to glorify Him in worship. Their work would become a lasting part of the worship of God's people as they offered their sacrifices and prayers at the tabernacle generation after generation.

Spiritual Insight:

Bezalel and those he trained were commissioned to a very noble calling, and they used their artistic skills to bring glory to God for generations to come. God continues to endow His people with gifts for the purpose of glorifying Himself and leading others to glorify Him as well (1 Corinthians 12; Romans 12). How might you use the gifts God has given you to glorify Him and lead others to do the same?

Meaning:
In the shadow of God

First Reference:
Exodus 31:2

Last Reference:
2 Chronicles 1:5

Boaz

WEALTHY BETHLEHEMITE WHO MARRIED WIDOWED RUTH

Now Naomi had a relative on her husband's side, a man of standing from the clan of Elimelek, whose name was Boaz.
RUTH 2:1 NIV

It is often in the smaller, less noticeable things we do that our true character is revealed. Do we impatiently stare at the checkout clerk working the long line ahead of us? Do we decide not to help with the new church ministry because we don't like the person in charge?

Surely Boaz faced similar decisions in his everyday life, but the Bible details various ways he showed unselfishness and concern for others—even at his own expense.

The book of Ruth recounts how Boaz, a farmer in Bethlehem, was a wealthy man, yet he took time to talk to others, such as his harvesters. He also took special notice of a young woman named Ruth who was gleaning in his fields, and he learned that she was the daughter-in-law of Naomi, the widow of his deceased relative Elimelech. Boaz made sure Ruth was protected and treated honorably while she gleaned in his fields. He provided her with abundant food and water and even instructed his men to purposely leave stalks of grain for her to gather.

Later Ruth appealed to Boaz that he marry her and purchase the land that had belonged to Naomi's husband so it would remain within the family. Boaz was certainly interested, but honorably and selflessly presented the offer first to a relative who was more closely related to Naomi. When the other relative declined, Boaz gladly acquired the land and Ruth as his wife.

Boaz and Ruth later had a son, Obed, who became an ancestor of David and ultimately an ancestor of Christ.

Related Information:

By purchasing the land and marrying Ruth, Boaz acted in the Old Testament role of kinsman-redeemer. In ancient Israel, God's covenant with His people included the offer of a portion of the Promised Land as an inheritance, so it was critical that everything be done to prevent the loss of one's land. The kinsman-redeemer could help a struggling relative by purchasing his or her land to ensure that it remained with the family.

Meaning:

--

First Reference:

Ruth 2:1

Last Reference:

1 Chronicles 2:12

Key References:

Ruth 2:8–16; 4:9–11

caiaphas

High Priest

But one of them, Caiaphas, who was high priest that year, said to them, "You know nothing at all. Nor do you understand that it is better for you that one man should die for the people, not that the whole nation should perish."
John 11:49–50 esv

Few things turn people's stomachs more than the abuse of power by religious leaders. Such people ought to be examples of godly, servant leadership—so when we see them clutching power and using it to serve themselves, we naturally feel angry and disgusted. Caiaphas certainly turned more than a few stomachs in his day, because it seems he was willing to do anything to retain his power.

Caiaphas was high priest and a member of the Jewish ruling council called the Sanhedrin. As Jesus grew in popularity and His miracles became well known, the religious leaders began to fear that the Romans would become involved. Caiaphas offered a simple solution: kill Jesus so the rest of the nation—and no doubt his own power over it—wasn't destroyed. Caiaphas's solution eventually culminated in the crucifixion of Jesus (Matthew 26:3–4, 57; John 11:47–53).

Later, when Peter and John healed a man who was crippled at the temple, the religious leaders, including Caiaphas, became involved again. Peter boldly told the leaders that he and John had performed the miracle by the authority of Jesus Christ, whom the leaders had put to death. Even though the leaders recognized that their miracle was impossible to deny, they threatened Peter and John to keep them from talking about Jesus (Acts 3–4)!

Did You Know?

In 1990 twelve ossuaries—bone boxes—of the family tomb of a "Caiaphas" were discovered two miles south of Jerusalem. It is possible that this was the same Caiaphas as the one who plotted Jesus' death.

Meaning:
The dell

First Reference:
Matthew 26:3

Last Reference:
Acts 4:6

15

CAIN

SON OF ADAM AND EVE

Cain said to his brother Abel, "Let us go out to the field."
And when they were in the field, Cain rose up against
his brother Abel, and killed him.
GENESIS 4:8 NRSV

Jealousy kills. And while Cain had intended only to kill his brother, the effects of his jealousy reached further than he could have imagined.

As the firstborn son of Adam and Eve, Cain became the third person to inhabit the earth. Together with his parents (and later his other brothers and sisters), Cain began to care for the earth and became a farmer (Genesis 4:2). But soon Cain—once the greatest achievement of Adam and Eve (Genesis 4:1)—became the scourge of his family when anger and jealousy drove him to murder his own brother. Not only did Cain's anger result in Abel's death, but it also brought painful consequences in his own life. God drove Cain away from his family to live as an outcast in the land of Nod. Cain's jealousy first destroyed his brother's life and the family's unity, and then it shattered his own life as well. First John 3:12 (NRSV) records, "We must not be like Cain who was from the evil one and murdered his brother. And why did he murder him? Because his own deeds were evil and his brother's righteous."

Although Cain showed no remorse for his crime, he still received God's gracious protection and was allowed to begin his own family and community in the land of Nod. Cain's sons and grandsons became the fathers of music, cattle keepers, and craftsmen who worked with bronze and iron (Genesis 4:22).

Did You Know?
The phrase, "Am I my brother's keeper?" originated with Cain. He said this to God after murdering his brother (Genesis 4:9).

Meaning:
Lance

First Reference:
Genesis 4:1

Last Reference:
Jude 1:11

Key References:
Genesis 4:9; Hebrews 11:4

CALEB

THE SPY WITH A "DIFFERENT" SPIRIT

*But my servant Caleb, because he has a different spirit and
has followed me fully, I will bring into the land into which
he went, and his descendants shall possess it.*
NUMBERS 14:24 ESV

The meaning of his name fit him well: *to rage with canine madness.* Just as a wild dog gives his undivided attention to ravenously attacking and devouring, so Caleb remained completely focused on God's command to take the Promised Land.

Sent to explore the land as one of the original twelve spies, Caleb (along with Joshua) tried to convince the people to carry out God's orders to take the land. When the people began to stray by following the counsel of the other ten spies, Caleb snapped, "'We should by all means go up and take possession of it, for we will surely overcome it'" (Numbers 13:30 NASB). His unyielding devotion and determination to the task was obvious throughout his life.

God rewarded Caleb's tenacity when He promised him a place in the Promised Land. Though millions of Hebrew people left slavery in Egypt, only two endured the forty years in the wilderness and entered the Promised Land: Joshua and Caleb (Numbers 14:30).

Even as an old man, Caleb's doggedness did not wane. Once the major battles wound down, an eighty-five-year-old Caleb approached Joshua and said, "I am still as strong today as I was in the day Moses sent me; as my strength was then, so my strength is now, for war and for going out and coming in. Now then, give me this hill country about which the LORD spoke on that day, for you heard on that day that Anakim were there, with great fortified cities; perhaps the LORD will be with me, and I will drive them out as the LORD has spoken" (Joshua 14:11–12 NASB). Joshua granted his request, and Caleb successfully settled the land of Hebron.

Did You Know?

By giving him the land of Hebron, Joshua rewarded Caleb's lifelong loyalty and devotion. Hebron, the city of the patriarchs, contained the tombs of Abraham, Sarah, Isaac, Jacob, Rebekah, and Leah.

Meaning:
Forcible

First Reference:
Numbers 13:6

Last Reference:
1 Chronicles 6:56

Key References:
Numbers 13:30; 32:11–12; Joshua 14:13

DANIEL

JEWISH PROPHET AND
ROYAL OFFICIAL OF BABYLON

*Then the king placed Daniel in a high position and lavished
many gifts on him. He made him ruler over the entire province
of Babylon and placed him in charge of all its wise men.*
DANIEL 2:48 NIV

Of all the people mentioned in scripture, few are spoken of
as highly as Daniel. Daniel probably came from the nobil-
ity of Judah, and he was a very young man when he was taken
into exile in Babylon. Despite his traumatic beginnings, however, Daniel prospered—both as an official in the Babylonian
royal court and as a follower of God.

Daniel first served in the court of Nebuchadnezzar along
with his friends Hananiah (Shadrach), Mishael (Meshach),
and Azariah (Abednego), and quickly distinguished himself by
his great learning and understanding. Later Daniel interpreted
various dreams for Nebuchadnezzar and was rewarded with
promotions and wealth. Daniel also interpreted a divine message given to Nebuchadnezzar's son Belshazzar.

Daniel continued his distinguished government service
even after the kingdom changed hands to the Persians. Yet his
devotion to God remained unshaken, as demonstrated by the
fact that it was his regular times of prayer that were used by
his enemies to trap him. With God's help, Daniel survived the
ordeal unscathed and continued to prosper.

Daniel was also a prophet who received several visions from God, mostly about the future rise and fall of various world powers.

Related Information:

Daniel's fame as a righteous and wise person must have been widely known even in his own day, because the prophet Ezekiel, who also lived in Babylon during the exile, spoke of Daniel's righteousness and wisdom three times in his book (Ezekiel 14:14, 20; 28:3).

Meaning:
Judge of God

First Reference:
Ezekiel 14:14

Last Reference:
Mark 13:14

Key References:
Daniel 1:8, 17; 2:31–45; 6:22–23

18

David

King of Israel

"But now your [Saul's] kingdom will not endure; the Lord has sought out a man after his own heart and appointed him ruler of his people, because you have not kept the Lord's command."
1 Samuel 13:14 NIV

Whether it's a eulogy at a funeral or a bit of reminiscing at the dinner table, it always seems like the best things are said about people when they are not around to hear it. In David's case, God's highest praise of him was spoken not to David but to Saul when the Lord was rebuking him for his unfaithfulness.

Understandably, David is famous for many things throughout his life—mostly good but some bad. As a boy, he killed the giant Goliath and played the harp to soothe Saul's troubled spirit. Later he was forced to flee from Saul when Saul tried to kill him. After David assumed the throne of Israel, he fought a number of battles and established Israel as the dominant power in the region.

Still later, David committed adultery with Bathsheba and arranged for her husband's death. After he repented, David made preparations to build a new temple to replace the tent that housed the ark of the covenant, although it was actually his son Solomon who built the temple. All the while, David composed psalms expressing his love for God and calling on God to rescue him from his enemies.

So was God's highest praise of David about one of David's

many accomplishments? Or about his skillful composition of praise songs? No. It was simply that David was "a man after [God's] own heart" (1 Samuel 13:14 NASB). That is what made David truly great in the eyes of God.

Spiritual Insight:

As we strive to honor God in life, what should be our highest aspiration? That we accomplish great things for God? That we live a godly life? Certainly these are noble goals. But ultimately our chief concern should be that we seek to have a heart that reflects the heart of God. No other praise could be greater.

Meaning:
Loving

First Reference:
Ruth 4:17

Last Reference:
Revelation 22:16

Key References:
1 Samuel 16:13; 18:6–9; 24:6–7; 2 Samuel 12:13; 22

DEBORah

PROPHETESS AND JUDGE OF ISRAEL

*And Deborah said to Barak, "Up! For this is the day in which
the LORD has given Sisera into your hand. Does not the LORD
go out before you?" So Barak went down from Mount Tabor
with 10,000 men following him.*
JUDGES 4:14 ESV

Deborah was a woman who knew what needed to be done and wasn't afraid to tell people. And apparently it was obvious to everyone else that she knew what she was talking about, because they listened.

We first read about Deborah, who was married to a man named Lappidoth, when she was leading the Israelites as a prophetess. She had set up her court in the hill country of Ephraim, roughly in the middle of the nation, and people came to her to have their disputes settled (Judges 4:4–5).

At some point, the Lord made it clear to Deborah that a man named Barak in the northern part of Israel was supposed to lead the Israelites to fight against the Canaanites who lived near him. When she told Barak, he must have gotten cold feet—but he trusted Deborah, because he refused to go into battle unless she went with him (Judges 4:7–8). Deborah agreed to go, but she warned Barak that, as a result, he would forfeit the glory for the victory. In the end, Deborah and Barak won a great victory over the Canaanites, and they celebrated by singing a victory song together.

Did You Know?

The hill country of Ephraim, where Deborah set up her court, was home to several other early leaders of Israel. The judge Ehud lived there (Judges 3), as did the judge/prophet Samuel (1 Samuel 7:15–17) and the first king, Saul (1 Samuel 9:1–4).

Meaning:

Bee

First Reference:

Judges 4:4

Last Reference:

Judges 5:15

DELILAH

WOMAN WHO LEARNED THE SECRET OF SAMSON'S STRENGTH

When Delilah saw that [Samson] had told her everything,
she sent word to the rulers of the Philistines, "Come back once more;
he has told me everything." So the rulers of the Philistines
returned with the silver in their hands.
JUDGES 16:18 NIV

From stealing petty cash at work to selling illegal drugs, some people will do anything for money. Delilah was even willing to hand over her lover, Samson, to his worst enemies.

Delilah lived in the Valley of Sorek during the time of the judges of Israel, when powerful Samson was wreaking havoc on the Philistines. This key valley linked the Israelites with their enemies the Philistines, so it was a constant area of conflict. The Bible doesn't say if Delilah was a Philistine or an Israelite, but she proved to be disloyal to Samson and harmful to Israel as a result (Judges 16).

Samson was an Israelite and a Nazirite from birth, meaning he had been specially dedicated to God and was not allowed to cut his hair or drink alcohol (Judges 13:3–5). Samson fell in love with Delilah, and the Philistine rulers immediately saw an opportunity to get to Samson. They offered to pay her a huge sum of money if she would tell them the secret of Samson's strength. She agreed and tried three times to get Samson to tell his secret, but he lied to her each time. Finally, he agreed to tell her where his strength came from: his Nazirite vow, which was confirmed by his long hair.

Delilah sent word to the Philistines, who came and cut Samson's hair while he slept. When Samson awoke, his amazing strength was gone, and the Philistines took him away captive. Eventually he would regain his strength for one last act, which would destroy many Philistines as well as himself.

Related Information:
Several other people in the Bible appear to have taken Nazirite vows for some or even all of their lives, including Samuel (1 Samuel 1–2), John the Baptist (Luke 1:13–17), and possibly even Paul (Acts 18:18; 21:23).

Meaning:
Languishing

First Reference:
Judges 16:4

Last Reference:
Judges 16:18

DORCAS

DISCIPLE WHOM PETER RAISED
FROM THE DEAD

*In Joppa there was a disciple named Tabitha (in Greek her name
is Dorcas); she was always doing good and helping the poor.*
ACTS 9:36 NIV

Dorcas was a continual witness to the power of God at work
in her life, from her generosity with her possessions, to her
own labors of love, to her amazing experience of being raised
to life again by Peter.

Dorcas, also known as Tabitha, lived in the town of Joppa,
one of the few port cities of Israel. The Bible describes her as a
disciple who was known and loved as a very generous woman
toward the poor. She made clothing for others and was always
doing good.

While Peter was ministering in the city of Lydda nearby,
Dorcas became sick and died—and some believers brought Peter to see what had happened. When he arrived, some widows
were mourning her death and showed Peter some clothes that
Dorcas had made for them.

Peter sent everyone from the room and prayed to God.
Then he turned to Dorcas, telling her to get up—and she did!
News of this amazing miracle spread throughout Joppa, and
many people believed in the Lord.

Related Information:

Dorcas's generous gifts of clothing for others are made even more admirable when we realize that clothing was typically much more expensive in ancient times than it is today. The making of cloth and clothing was essentially an entirely manual process, so it took a long time to make a single item. As a result, clothing was expensive, and people could not usually afford many sets of clothing.

Meaning:

Gazelle

First Reference:

Acts 9:36

Last Reference:

Acts 9:39

ELI

PRIEST OF ISRAEL

*Now the young man Samuel was ministering to the LORD
under Eli. And the word of the LORD was rare in those days;
there was no frequent vision.*
1 SAMUEL 3:1 ESV

It's a classic model: an enthusiastic visionary founds an organization and steers it to excellence, but over time the organization is drained dry as less dedicated leadership allows things to grow more and more lax. That must have been the general tenor of things by the time Eli's priestly ministry in Shiloh was winding down.

Eli himself is not necessarily spoken of in scripture as corrupt or sinful, but it appears that he had let his own sons, who also served as priests, become very corrupt and abusive of their office (1 Samuel 2:10–18). Because of this, Eli's family was cursed by God—and this may be the reason that few people received special messages or visions from the Lord (1 Samuel 2:27–36).

In the meantime, God was raising up Samuel to replace Eli's sons as priests and leaders of the people. Samuel had been brought to Shiloh as a young boy and left in the care of Eli (1 Samuel 2–3). The final blow to Eli's family came when the Israelites were fighting against the Philistines. Both of Eli's sons were killed as they carried the ark of the covenant into battle, and even Eli himself fell over backward and broke his neck when he heard the news that the ark had been captured (1 Samuel 4).

Spiritual Insight:

It is very shortsighted to think that all we need to concern ourselves with is our own spiritual walk. This attitude leaves the spiritual lives of those who come after us in jeopardy. What are we doing to promote faithfulness to God in the lives of our children and others entrusted to our care?

Meaning:
Lofty

First Reference:
1 Samuel 1:3

Last Reference:
1 Kings 2:27

Key References:
1 Samuel 1:13–14; 2:29; 3:8–9

ELiJah

PROPHET OF ISRAEL

[Elijah] replied, "I have been very zealous for the LORD God Almighty. The Israelites have rejected your covenant, torn down your altars, and put your prophets to death with the sword. I am the only one left, and now they are trying to kill me too."
1 KINGS 19:14 NIV

Even the greatest of God's servants can become overwhelmed by circumstances. Just ask Elijah, God's prophet to Israel during the evil reign of King Ahab.

Elijah was called by God to prophesy against the wickedness of Ahab and the Israelites during one of the darkest times in its history. King Ahab and his wife, Jezebel, had been promoting idolatry throughout the land and were trying to rid the land of the prophets of the Lord. Elijah faithfully and courageously confronted Ahab repeatedly about his sins and witnessed various miracles from God.

Perhaps the greatest confrontation between Elijah and Ahab took place on Mount Carmel. There Elijah called for hundreds of the prophets of Baal and Asherah to meet him and see which God or gods answered their prayers to consume a sacrifice. When Elijah's God proved victorious over the other gods, Elijah instructed the people to kill all the prophets of Baal and Asherah.

Having just witnessed this amazing miracle, however, Elijah fled for his life to Horeb (Mount Sinai) to escape the wrath of Jezebel. Along the way, and even while he was there speaking with God, Elijah expressed despair that he was the only one left who worshipped God.

God answered him by giving him some very direct commands of what to do next, and He assured him that he was not alone, for there were still seven thousand others in Israel who refused to bow down to idols. Elijah obeyed and anointed Elisha to succeed him in his ministry.

Spiritual Insight:

When you feel overwhelmed in your walk with God, take heart in knowing that God is always in control—and He can raise up others to help even when it seems that no one else cares about God.

Meaning:
God of Jehovah

First Reference:
1 Kings 17:1

Last Reference:
James 5:17

Key References:
1 Kings 17:1–6; 18:21–40; 2 Kings 2:11

ELizaBETh

MOTHER OF JOHN THE BAPTIST

When it was time for Elizabeth to have her baby, she gave birth
to a son. Her neighbors and relatives heard that the Lord
had shown her great mercy, and they shared her joy.
LUKE 1:57–58 NIV

Few joys in life are felt as deeply as that of a mother who is blessed with a child after many years of struggling to become pregnant. This was the wonderful experience of Elizabeth, and we are privileged to share in her joy year after year as we read the scriptures surrounding the Christmas story.

Elizabeth was the wife of a priest named Zechariah, and both of them served God blamelessly. Elizabeth was also a relative of Mary, who would later give birth to Jesus.

When we first read about Elizabeth and her husband, they are already very old, and they have been unable to bear any children (Luke 1:5–7).

But once, while Zechariah was on duty in the temple, an angel appeared to him and announced that Elizabeth would have a son, and they were to name him John (whom we know as "John the Baptist").

About the same time, an angel appeared to Mary and announced that she would give birth to Jesus and that Elizabeth would also bear a child. When Mary went to visit Elizabeth, Elizabeth was filled with the Holy Spirit, and her child leaped in her womb. In a wonderful testament of faith and humility,

Elizabeth asked, "'Why am I so favored, that the mother of my Lord should come to me?'" (Luke 1:43 NIV).

Elizabeth did indeed give birth to a son, and they named him John, as the angel had instructed. All her neighbors and relatives shared in her great joy.

Related Information:

Mary's visit to Elizabeth was no small event. She was already expecting a child, and it would have taken her about three days to travel from Nazareth to the hills of Judea. She then stayed with Elizabeth for about three months before making the same journey back to Nazareth—three months further along in her pregnancy (Luke 1:39, 56).

Meaning:
God of the oath

First Reference:
Luke 1:5

Last Reference:
Luke 1:57

Elymas

JEWISH SORCERER BLINDED BY PAUL

*But Elymas the magician (for that is the meaning of this name)
opposed them, seeking to turn the proconsul away from the faith.*
ACTS 13:8 ESV

The short story of Elymas (also called Bar-Jesus), which
takes up a mere seven verses of scripture (Acts 13:6–12), is
filled with contrasts from start to finish.

Paul and Barnabas encountered Elymas at Paphos after
traveling through the island of Cyprus. Elymas, a Jewish sorcerer and false prophet, was an attendant of the Roman proconsul in Paphos. As Paul and Barnabas tried to share the truth
of the gospel with the proconsul, Elymas tried to turn him
from the faith. So Paul rebuked Elymas and told him that the
Lord was going to blind him for a time, which is exactly what
happened. After that, the proconsul was amazed and believed
in the Lord.

Three stark contrasts stand out in the story: First, as a Jew,
Elymas was supposed to worship the Lord and refrain from
practicing divination and sorcery (Leviticus 19:26; Deuteronomy 18:10–13; Ezekiel 13:9, 20; Micah 3:6–7), yet he was
doing these very things in the service of the Roman proconsul.
Second, Elymas was characterized by deceit and trickery (Acts
13:10), yet he wanted to turn the proconsul from the truth of
the gospel. And third, Elymas was no doubt employed by the
proconsul, because he offered special knowledge and power

through sorcery—yet in the end Elymas himself was blinded and needed to be led by the hand.

Related Information:

Elymas is described in the Bible as a "sorcerer," which is actually the Greek word *magos*. This is the same word (plural, *magi*) used for the "wise men" who came from the East, probably Persia or Babylonia, to worship the young Jesus (Matthew 2:1–2). By Roman times, magi had become associated with magic and divination, and many of them had flocked to the Roman Empire to profit from their practices.

Meaning:
--

Only Reference:
Acts 13:8

ENoch

MAN WHO WALKED WITH GOD

Enoch walked with God; and he was not, for God took him.
GENESIS 5:24 NASB

There are some things in the Bible we will likely never fully understand until we get to eternity. The single, simple, yet puzzling statement in Genesis 5:24 regarding Enoch's experience with God is undoubtedly one of them.

What does it mean that Enoch "walked with God"? What does it mean that God "took him" away? Scholars and laypersons alike have pondered the exact meaning of these words for thousands of years, but no one knows for sure. Most believe that "walked with God" means that he lived a godly life in close communion with God. As a result, Enoch was translated straight to heaven without experiencing death (see Hebrews 11:5).

Besides genealogies, the only other places Enoch is mentioned in the Bible are Hebrews 11:5, where he is commended as a man of faith who pleased God, and Jude 1:14, where he is said to have prophesied regarding the Lord's return.

Are you interested in growing in your spiritual life? Spend time contemplating what it might have meant for Enoch to "walk with God"—and incorporate some of those traits into your own life.

Related Information:

Beginning a few hundred years before the birth of Jesus Christ, several works were written as prophecies of Enoch. Some of these were included in certain versions of the Bible, such as the Ethiopic Bible and the Old Slavonic Bible. It is likely that one of these books, commonly called 1 Enoch, is the one referred to by Jude (though this does not imply that 1 Enoch is inspired scripture), and the books of 1 Peter and Revelation may draw imagery from this book as well.

Meaning:
Initiated

First Reference:
Genesis 5:18

Last Reference:
Jude 1:14

ESAU

BROTHER OF JACOB

But Esau ran to meet him and embraced him and
fell on his neck and kissed him, and they wept.
GENESIS 33:4 ESV

Often, just when you think you know someone, that person does something completely unexpected, and you're left scratching your head trying to make sense of it all. Esau must have been someone like that.

Esau was the older twin brother of Jacob; they were the sons of Isaac and grandsons of Abraham. As the oldest sibling, Esau was entitled to the family birthright, which granted him leadership of the extended family and a double portion of his father's inheritance. But Esau revealed his disregard for his birthright when he sold it to Jacob for a bowl of stew. Later Jacob made sure to seal the deal by tricking his father into blessing him as the one receiving the birthright (Genesis 25–27).

When Esau realized that his birthright was lost forever, he became furious with Jacob and wanted to kill him. So Jacob fled far away to Paddan Aram (Genesis 27:42–28:5).

After many years, Jacob returned to Canaan, and along the way he heard that Esau was coming to meet him. Jacob feared for his life, thinking that Esau was still looking to exact revenge on him for stealing the birthright. When Esau caught up with him, however, he ran to Jacob and kissed him! The two brothers were finally reconciled (Genesis 32–33).

Related Information:

Esau became the ancestor of the Edomites, who lived in the mountainous area to the southeast of Israel (Genesis 36:9). The rivalry between Jacob and Esau appears to have continued through their descendants, the Israelites and the Edomites. The Israelites fought several battles with the Edomites throughout their history (2 Samuel 8:13; 2 Kings 8:21; 14:1–7).

Meaning:
Rough

First Reference:
Genesis 25:25

Last Reference:
Hebrews 12:16

Key References:
Genesis 25:30–33; 27:41; 36:6–8

28

ESThER

QUEEN OF PERSIA

"For if you [Esther] remain silent at this time, relief and deliverance for the Jews will arise from another place, but you and your father's family will perish. And who knows but that you have come to your royal position for such a time as this?"
ESTHER 4:14 NIV

Whether it's a fan catching a home run baseball in the World Series or a parent catching her child as she falls off a swing set, so much of life is about being at the right place at the right time. Queen Esther seemed to be at the right place and the right time to save her people, the Jews. Would she risk her life to try?

Esther was a Jew living in the mighty Persian Empire, which stretched from the borders of India to the borders of Europe. Many years earlier, Jews had been exiled from their homeland of Israel and scattered throughout places that would eventually be engulfed by the Persian Empire. Esther had been chosen by the king of Persia as his new queen, but she was still only allowed to come into his presence if it pleased him to do so.

When wicked Haman, a high official in the Persian Empire, devised a plan to eradicate all Jews, Esther's relative urged her to take advantage of her privileged position in the empire to save her people. At the risk of her life, she approached the king and invited him to a banquet, where she revealed Haman's plot. The king executed Haman and saved the Jews by allowing them to defend themselves against those who tried to carry out Haman's plan.

Spiritual Insight:

We'll probably never be faced with saving God's people from total eradication—but we all encounter situations where we are placed in the right place at the right time to do something for God. Whether it is giving part of a bonus to missions or spending a free evening helping out with a church youth group event, look for opportunities to make a lasting impact on God's kingdom with the resources you have been given.

Meaning:

--

First Reference:

Esther 2:7

Last Reference:

Esther 9:32

Key Reference:

Esther 4:14–16

ETHIOPIAN EUNUCH

OFFICIAL MET BY PHILIP

*So [Philip] started out, and on his way he met an Ethiopian eunuch,
an important official in charge of all the treasury of the Kandake
(which means "queen of the Ethiopians"). This man had
gone to Jerusalem to worship.*
ACTS 8:27 NIV

Once in a great while it happens. Someone begins asking us
questions about God or the gospel, and before we know
it, he or she has virtually rolled out the red carpet to be led to
Christ. That's the situation with the Ethiopian eunuch whom
Philip encountered on the road to Gaza.

Ethiopia was the same country that was called Cush in the
Old Testament. It was located south of Egypt in Africa, hundreds of miles from Israel. During the time of the Babylonian
conquest of Judah, many Jews fled to Ethiopia to escape. Their
influence may have been what led to a large following of native
Ethiopians to worship the God of Israel.

By the time of the New Testament, Ethiopia had been
ruled by several queens, all taking the title Kandake—much
like the title Caesar of the Roman Empire. The eunuch was an
official of this kingdom, and he had just been to Jerusalem to
worship there. The Lord led a Christian leader named Philip
to go down to Gaza, where he met the eunuch reading the
scriptures in his chariot. As they began to talk, the eunuch
asked Philip to explain who was being talked about in Isaiah

53—and Philip told him that this referred to Jesus. The eunuch became a believer, and then he was baptized. Philip was then led by the Spirit to Azotus, and the eunuch went on his way rejoicing (Acts 8:26–40).

Related Information:

Though it is only speculation, it is possible that the Ethiopian eunuch was actually looking for a passage in Isaiah 56:3–4, and he may have only unrolled the scroll as far as chapter 53 by the time Philip met him.

Meaning:

--

First Reference:
Acts 8:27

Last Reference:
Acts 8:39

EVE

THE FIRST WOMAN AND MOTHER OF ALL PEOPLE

*When the woman saw that the fruit of the tree was good for
food and pleasing to the eye, and also desirable for gaining wisdom,
she took some and ate it. She also gave some to her husband,
who was with her, and he ate it.*
GENESIS 3:6 NIV

It's sobering to realize that a lifetime of goodness can be forever marred by a single sin or poor decision, and the consequences can be seemingly immeasurable. In the case of Eve, the consequences of her sin affected the entire world for the rest of time.

As most people know, Eve was the first woman, created by God from a rib from Adam's side. She and Adam lived in a beautiful garden in perfect harmony with God and with the rest of creation—until she and Adam chose to disobey and eat from the one tree that they were forbidden to eat from in all the garden.

Certainly when Eve ate the fruit, she never imagined all the harm that her sin would cause. Yet that is the nature of sin. It looks pleasing and harmless, but the final result is always death. No amount of blaming each other or the serpent, who tempted her to eat the fruit, could change the sad consequences that would forever plague Adam and Eve and all their descendants. Forced to leave the garden, their lives—and the lives of all who have come after them—would now be marked by hard work, pain, and sorrow.

Related Information:

After Adam and Eve were forced to leave the garden, Eve gave birth to Cain and Abel. Years later, Cain killed Abel out of jealousy, but God gave Eve another son named Seth. Eve likely had other sons and daughters as well (Genesis 5:4).

Meaning:

Life-giver

First Reference:

Genesis 3:20

Last Reference:

1 Timothy 2:13

EZEKIEL

PROPHET OF JUDAH

*"Son of man, behold, I am about to take the delight of
your eyes away from you at a stroke; yet you shall
not mourn or weep, nor shall your tears run down."*
EZEKIEL 24:16 ESV

How do you speak truth to people who have no interest in
hearing it? This was as much a dilemma in the time of Ezekiel as it is today. And the solution was the same then as it is
today: We speak with our lives.

Ezekiel was a priest who was taken into exile in Babylon
along with many other people of Judah (Ezekiel 1:3). For many
years he prophesied to the people in Babylon, giving them
messages of both condemnation and hope. The Lord called
him to tell the people that they were in Babylon because they
had sinned greatly against the Lord—and Ezekiel often used
very harsh words and powerful illustrations to make the people
listen. There were times, though, when it seemed the only thing
people would heed was Ezekiel's very own life before them.

Perhaps the most moving life-message that Ezekiel gave
the people was a warning of the destruction that awaited Jerusalem. The Lord told Ezekiel that his wife, "the delight of [his]
eyes," would soon die—and Ezekiel was not to publicly mourn
her death. Instead, he would only be allowed to grieve within
himself. This prophecy foretold how God was about to destroy
Jerusalem, the delight of the people's eyes, and they would not

be free to mourn over the city but would waste away inside, reflecting on their own sins. Only after Ezekiel and his people had been notified of the city's destruction would Ezekiel be allowed to speak.

Spiritual Insight:

In terms of people's hearts, we live in a world that is not all that different from the world of Ezekiel's day. People's hearts have been hardened by sin, and their eyes have been blinded to the truth. The only message that many people will ever willingly accept is the testimony of our lives. What message about God is your life communicating?

Meaning:
God will strengthen

First Reference:
Ezekiel 1:3

Last Reference:
Ezekiel 24:24

GIDEON

JUDGE OF ISRAEL

And he said to him, "Please, Lord, how can I save Israel? Behold, my
clan is the weakest in Manasseh, and I am the least in my father's
house." And the LORD said to him, "But I will be with you, and you
shall strike the Midianites as one man."
JUDGES 6:15–16 ESV

In a world weaned on the idea that success comes to those who
believe in themselves, Gideon is a welcome misfit. Believing in
himself—or even in the power of God for that matter—seemed
virtually foreign to Gideon before God used him to do great
things.

During a time when the Midianites were oppressing God's
people, the Lord appeared to Gideon and told him to rescue
His people—but Gideon responded pessimistically with, "How
can I save Israel? Behold, my clan is the weakest in Manasseh,
and I am the least in my father's house" (Judges 6:15 ESV).
When the Lord told him to tear down his father's pagan altar,
Gideon did so—but at night out of fear of his family and the
townspeople. As Gideon prepared to fight the Midianites, he
asked God two different times to send a sign to confirm that
this was His will (Judges 6:34–40).

Even with Gideon's rather meek display of faith, however,
God used him to rout the Midianites. And apparently in the
process, God wanted to teach Gideon a lesson in faith—because
He whittled Gideon's army down from thirty-two thousand to

three hundred before the battle took place. In the end, Israel was rescued from the Midianites, and Gideon became a judge over the people for the rest of his life.

Spiritual Insight:

Gideon is living proof that it is not the greatness of our faith that makes the difference but the greatness of the One in whom we have faith. Likewise, Jesus once said, "If you have faith as small as a mustard seed, you can say to this mountain, 'Move from here to there,' and it will move. Nothing will be impossible for you" (Matthew 17:20 NIV). Take courage in the great God in whom we believe.

Meaning:
Warrior

First Reference:
Judges 6:11

Last Reference:
Judges 8:35

Key References:
Judges 6:11; 7:6–7, 20–22

GOLIATH

PHILISTINE WARRIOR KILLED BY DAVID

*And there came out from the camp of the Philistines a champion
named Goliath of Gath, whose height was six cubits and a span.*
1 SAMUEL 17:4 ESV

It's often who you know that makes all the difference. From
business to politics to box seats at sold-out sporting events,
making a simple connection to an important name is sometimes all you need to go from zero to a dream come true. But
the key, of course, is *who*—whose name are you able to drop?

Goliath, a giant from the Philistine city of Gath, mistak-
enly assumed that the only names he needed were those of his
people and his pagan gods (1 Samuel 17:8, 43).When the Philistines were preparing for battle against the Israelites, Goliath
presented himself as the Philistines' champion and challenged
the Israelites to send their own champion to fight him in order
to determine which group would be victorious. He identified
himself as a Philistine, and he wrongly assumed that all the
Israelite warriors were merely servants of Saul (1 Samuel 17:8).
But the shepherd boy David knew better. He came to Goliath
in the name of the Lord, and this name would make all the difference (1 Samuel 17:43–47).

The Lord gave David victory over Goliath and the other
Israelites victory over the Philistine army, and Goliath's
name—and the name of his gods—would forever be associated
with defeat.

Spiritual Insight:

God has promised that those who hope in Him will not be disappointed (Isaiah 49:23), for His name is above every name, and He is the only One with the power to rescue all who call on Him (Acts 4:12). Have you called on this name for your salvation?

Meaning:
Exile

First Reference:
1 Samuel 17:4

Last Reference:
1 Chronicles 20:5

Hagar,

Sarah's Maidservant and Mother of Ishmael

*And he said, "Hagar, slave of Sarai, where have you come from,
and where are you going?" "I'm running away
from my mistress Sarai," she answered.*
GENESIS 16:8 NIV

Have you ever felt so alone that it seemed like no one cared if you lived or died? Hagar knew these feelings—twice.

Hagar was the maidservant of Sarah (named Sarai at the time), the wife of Abraham. God had promised Abraham and Sarah that they would have many descendants, but because of her advanced age, Sarah had not been able to conceive. Sarah came up with her own plan B that involved the socially accepted practice of allowing her maidservant, Hagar, to conceive for her. After Hagar became pregnant with Abraham's child, however, she began to look down on Sarah, and Sarah began to mistreat her in return. Eventually Hagar fled into the desert to escape. Along the way, the Lord spoke to her and told her to return to Sarah, and He would raise up her child to be the father of a great nation—though that would not be the people of Israel.

A while after Hagar gave birth to Ishmael, Sarah became angry with her again, and this time Sarah sent her away into the desert with Ishmael. When Hagar ran out of water and prepared for Ishmael to die of thirst, the Lord appeared to her again and reiterated His promise to make Ishmael into a great nation. He also showed her a nearby well, and she and Ishmael were saved from certain death.

Spiritual Insight:

There are times when we will be mistreated by others, and we may feel like no one cares what happens to us—but God always sees us, and He always cares (Psalm 139).We can trust ourselves to Him and know that He is working for our good even in the midst of wrongs that we may be experiencing (Genesis 50:18–20; Romans 8).

Meaning:
--

First Reference:
Genesis 16:1

Last Reference:
Genesis 25:12

Key References:
Genesis 16:1–2, 15; 21:10

Haggai

PROPHET OF JUDEA AFTER THE EXILE

*Then Zerubbabel the son of Shealtiel, and Joshua the son of Jehozadak,
the high priest, with all the remnant of the people, obeyed the voice of
the LORD their God, and the words of Haggai the prophet, as the LORD
their God had sent him. And the people feared the LORD.*
HAGGAI 1:12 ESV

In a big game with only an inning or two left, every baseball
coach worth his salt knows to bring in his ace "closer," a
pitcher whose sole job is to stop the other team from scoring
runs and ensure victory. The prophet Haggai must have been an
amazing closer.

Many prophets had spent nearly their whole lives relaying
God's messages to His people but with little positive response.
Haggai's prophetic ministry, on the other hand, appears to have
spanned only four months, but by God's providence it resulted
in the completion of the second temple.

The first temple had been destroyed by the Babylonians
several decades earlier, and now many Jews had returned from
exile and had begun to rebuild the temple. The project had
been at a standstill for many years due to opposition from
hostile neighbors, but the Lord began to stir the hearts of the
Jewish leaders once again through the words of Haggai and
Zechariah. These two prophets called for the people to finish
what they had started, and the people responded.

Related Information:

Haggai may have been very old when he delivered his prophecies to God's people, because Haggai 2:3 seems to imply that he saw the first temple with his own eyes before it was destroyed. The first temple was destroyed over sixty-five years before Haggai delivered his messages.

Meaning:
Festive

First Reference:
Ezra 5:1

Last Reference:
Haggai 2:20

Key References:
Ezra 6:14; Haggai 2:9–10

36

Haman

Enemy of the Jews during Esther's Time

*And all the king's servants who were at the king's gate bowed
down and paid homage to Haman, for the king had so commanded
concerning him. But Mordecai did not bow down or pay homage.*
Esther 3:2 esv

From lying about our accomplishments to driving ourselves
into debt to "keep up with the Joneses," there is no limit
to what pride can make people do. Given enough opportunity,
pride could probably even lead us to do something even as sin-
ister as what Haman did.

Haman was a high government official in the mighty Persian Empire. The Persians ruled over virtually all the known
world at the time, including the land of Israel—and there were
many Jews living in Susa, the capital of the empire. Haman had
recently been bestowed with high honor within the government, and his heart was completely puffed up with pride. Everyone was required to bow in his presence.

When a Jew named Mordecai refused to bow down, Haman became furious and made plans to exterminate *all* the
Jews in the empire. Unbeknownst to Haman, however, the new
queen, Esther, was a Jew—and she was related to Mordecai.
When Mordecai and Esther learned of Haman's evil plot, the
queen hatched a plot herself to inform the king. At a grand
banquet hosted by the queen, she revealed Haman's wicked
plan to exterminate her people. In the end the Jews were saved,
and Haman and his sons were killed instead.

Spiritual Insight:

It may be tempting to think that we are above something so wicked as Haman's plot, but we are all susceptible to sin— any sin—and given the right circumstances we can be led to do things we never imagined we were capable of. What sins are lurking in your heart? Do you secretly harbor prideful thoughts? Sinful desires? Hateful grudges? Expose them in prayer before God and repent of them before your sins expose you and lead you to certain destruction.

Meaning:
--

First Reference:
Esther 3:1

Last Reference:
Esther 9:24

Key References:
Esther 3:5–11

HaNNah
MOTHER OF SAMUEL

In her deep anguish Hannah prayed to the LORD, weeping bitterly.
And she made a vow, saying, "LORD Almighty, if you will. . .
not forget your servant but give her a son, then I will give him
to the LORD for all the days of his life."
I SAMUEL 1:10–11 NIV

One of the most moving passages of scripture is the story of Hannah, the mother of the prophet Samuel. In the span of two simple chapters, we find such heartfelt themes as the pain and longing of childlessness, the joy of childbirth, and the surrender of a child to God's service.

When we first read about Hannah, she has been unable to bear a child and is being taunted for this by her rival, Peninnah, who is the other wife of Hannah's husband. Hannah's sorrow and longing lead her to pray earnestly to God for a son, whom she promises to dedicate fully to God's service (1 Samuel 1).

God answers Hannah's prayer, and she gives birth to Samuel. True to her word, Hannah brings Samuel to the tabernacle after he is weaned and gives him over to God's service there. Instead of expressing sorrow at her loss of Samuel, however, Hannah praises God for answering her prayer for a son (1 Samuel 2:1–10). Hannah eventually bears more children, and Samuel becomes a great prophet and judge over Israel.

Did You Know?

When Hannah promised to give her son over to God's service (1 Samuel 1:11), she was probably offering to make him a Nazirite for his entire life. People dedicated as Nazirites were not allowed to cut their hair or drink alcohol (Numbers 6).

Meaning:
Favored

First Reference:
1 Samuel 1:2

Last Reference:
1 Samuel 2:21

Key References:
1 Samuel 1:11, 15–16

HEROD THE GREAT

KING OF JUDEA

Then Herod, when he saw that he had been tricked by the wise men, became furious, and he sent and killed all the male children in Bethlehem and in all that region who were two years old or under, according to the time that he had ascertained from the wise men.
MATTHEW 2:16 ESV

Herod the Great was a man of many contradictions. He was king of Judea, yet he himself was an Idumean (that is, an Edomite). He gained favor with the Jewish leaders by completely renovating the temple of the Lord and making it rival any pagan temple of its day, yet he also built many pagan gymnasiums and other Hellenistic buildings throughout Judea and Samaria. He was often particular to maintain at least the appearance of conformity to Jewish customs, yet he freely broke the sixth commandment by mercilessly killing any who threatened his rule—including his own wife and sons. This contradiction led one ancient writer to comment that he would rather be Herod's *hus* ("pig," considered unfit to eat for Jews) than his *huios* ("son").

Herod's actions regarding Jesus' birth, then, should come as no surprise to us. When wise men came from the East seeking to worship the newborn King Jesus, they first asked Herod where the child was. Herod led them to believe that he wanted to worship the child, too, all the while planning to kill Him. When the wise men left without telling Herod exactly where the baby was, he became furious and ordered all the baby boys two years and younger to be killed. Jesus' family escaped to Egypt until Herod had died, then returned to Nazareth, where His parents had lived before He was born.

Related Information:

Several people were named Herod in the Bible. Herod the Great had several sons, including Antipas (who ruled over Galilee and Perea), Archelaus (who ruled over Judea and Samaria), and Philip (who ruled over the northeast corner of Palestine). Much later, Herod's grandson Agrippa ruled over much of Judea and Samaria, and still later Agrippa II ruled over portions of Palestine and Lebanon.

Meaning:
Heroic

First Reference:
Matthew 2:1

Last Reference:
Acts 23:35

HEZEKIAH

KING OF JUDAH

*[Hezekiah] held fast to the LORD and did not stop following him; he
kept the commands the LORD had given Moses. And the LORD was
with him; he was successful in whatever he undertook.*
2 KINGS 18:6–7 NIV

Just as the darkest backdrops make diamonds sparkle the
brightest, the dark days surrounding Hezekiah's reign made
his godly life all the more brilliant.

Hezekiah's own father had promoted idolatry throughout
Judah and had made Judah a subservient kingdom to the wicked
Assyrian Empire (2 Kings 16). When Hezekiah assumed the
throne of Judah at the age of twenty-five, the northern kingdom of Israel was only a few years away from being sent into
exile for their wickedness (2 Kings 18:9–10). These were dark
days indeed.

But Hezekiah determined to follow the Lord with all his
heart, and the Lord empowered him to do great things for
His people even in the midst of the evil forces that were still
at work. Hezekiah removed idolatry from the land, including
all the pagan items from the temple (2 Kings 18). He restored
proper worship at the temple and sent invitations to everyone
throughout the land—even people living in the northern kingdom of Israel—to come to Jerusalem to celebrate the Passover
once again (2 Chronicles 29–30).

Not long after the northern kingdom of Israel fell to the

Assyrians, the Assyrians attacked Jerusalem as well, but the Lord struck down 185,000 of their soldiers in a single night, and Jerusalem was spared (2 Kings 19:35–36).

Related Information:

As part of his preparations for the Assyrian attack on Jerusalem, Hezekiah constructed a water tunnel to carry water from the Gihon Spring to the pool at the lower end of the city (2 Kings 20:20). The tunnel still exists today, and in 1838 an ancient inscription was found in it that commemorated its construction.

Meaning:
Strengthened of God

First Reference:
2 Kings 16:20

Last Reference:
Micah 1:1

Key References:
2 Kings 18:1–7; 19:4–7; 20:9–11

40

Hosea

PROPHET OF ISRAEL

When the LORD began to speak through Hosea, the LORD said to him,
"Go, marry a promiscuous woman and have children with her, for like
an adulterous wife this land is guilty of unfaithfulness to the LORD."
HOSEA 1:2 NIV

If you have ever looked through the personals section of the newspaper, it's unlikely that you found someone seeking "unfaithful female, likely to have affairs." Who would want to marry someone like that? Yet that's exactly the kind of woman God told Hosea to marry as an object lesson about Israel's un-faithfulness to God.

Hosea was a prophet to the northern kingdom of Israel, and his intimate knowledge of that land suggests he was prob-ably from there. At some point in his life, God commanded him to marry an adulterous wife, and she bore him three chil-dren (Hosea 1). It is not known for certain whether his wife, named Gomer, was adulterous when Hosea married her or whether she only became unfaithful after their wedding. In any case, Hosea demonstrated unrelenting love for Gomer even af-ter she left him for another lover. He went so far as to buy her back from her lover and offered her a chance to be faithful to him once again (Hosea 3:1–2).

All Hosea's actions toward Gomer served to illustrate what God experienced with Israel, His covenant partner. Though God was faithful to Israel, the people were unfaithful to Him and chose to give themselves over to idolatry and wickedness. God sought to bring them back by sending prophets to warn them of the consequences of their sin.

Related Information:

Hosea 11:1 (NIV) says, "When Israel was a child, I loved him, and out of Egypt I called my son." There it refers to the Exodus, when Israel was led out of Egypt to follow the Lord and establish a new nation in Canaan. The Gospel of Matthew quotes this same verse to explain why Jesus' family was forced to flee to Egypt to escape Herod (Matthew 2:15).

Meaning:
Deliverer

First Reference:
Hosea 1:1

Last Reference:
Hosea 1:6

Isaac

SON OF ABRAHAM AND FATHER OF JACOB

*Isaac reopened the wells that had been dug in the time of his father
Abraham, which the Philistines had stopped up after Abraham died,
and he gave them the same names his father had given them.*
GENESIS 26:18 NIV

In a world that celebrates pioneers and trailblazers, it is easy to
underestimate the importance of those who faithfully carry
on what others have established. But a brief look at the life of
Isaac, the son of Abraham and father of Jacob, will show that
such people are just as critical to God's plan as those who are
marking a new trail for others.

Isaac's greatest claim to fame was simply that he was the
son of Abraham and Sarah, the child that was promised by the
Lord to carry on Abraham's name and make him into a great
nation.

As a young man, Isaac was nearly sacrificed by his father
in a test of obedience, but at the last second the Lord stopped
Abraham and showed him a ram to sacrifice instead. Later
Abraham acquired a wife for Isaac from Haran, the land of his
ancestors, and Isaac and Rebekah gave birth to the twins Esau
and Jacob.

Much of Isaac's adult life consisted simply of maintain-
ing and bolstering the abundance handed down to him by his
father. He continued to look after his extensive herds of livestock, and he repeatedly reopened wells that his father had dug

that had been stopped up by jealous neighbors.

In his later years, Isaac bestowed his blessing on his sons and unwittingly granted the greater blessing of birthright to the younger son, Jacob, who had deceived him into thinking he was the older son.

Spiritual Insight:

It is often tempting to think that we are nothing if we are not making waves. But the simple faithfulness of Isaac makes it clear that some of us are simply called to be devoted followers and faithful managers of the things handed down by others. Make a point to appreciate the role such people play, whether that be your role or the role of others around you.

Meaning:
Laughter

First Reference:
Genesis 17:19

Last Reference:
James 2:21

Key References:
Genesis 22:7–9; 24:3–4; 25:19–34

42

Isaiah

PROPHET OF ISRAEL AND JUDAH

Then I [Isaiah] said, "For how long, Lord?" And he answered: "Until the cities lie ruined and without inhabitant, until the houses are left deserted and the fields ruined and ravaged, until the LORD has sent everyone far away and the land is utterly forsaken."
ISAIAH 6:11–12 NIV

Wanted: dedicated employee who will faithfully proclaim messages of judgment to people who will reject and despise you. All efforts will produce little noticeable results and will end in complete destruction." It's unlikely that a job posting like that would garner many applicants. Yet that is essentially the job to which the prophet Isaiah was called by God.

Isaiah was probably closely affiliated with the royal court, given his relatively easy access to the king (Isaiah 7:3). But at some point in his life, the Lord, in His royal splendor, appeared to him in a vision (Isaiah 6), and Isaiah's life was forever changed. He was called to prophesy God's messages of judgment and restoration to His people, but God also warned him that the people would not listen and would eventually experience destruction. Even Isaiah's own children bore prophetic names: Shear-Jashub ("A Remnant Shall Return") and Maher-Shalal-Hash-Baz ("Swift Is Spoil, Speedy Is Prey").

Isaiah faithfully carried out his solemn and weighty task to the very end. He began prophesying a few decades before the fall of the northern kingdom of Israel and ended a few decades after this event.

Isaiah's efforts were not really futile, though, for his words were recorded for later generations in the book of Isaiah. Many of these prophecies foretold the Messiah, who would redeem His people from their bondage.

Related Information:

Isaiah is the Old Testament book most quoted in the New Testament. Jesus quoted Isaiah 6:9–10, which speaks of the people's callous hearts, when His disciples asked why He spoke in parables rather than in direct statements (Matthew 13:13–15).

Meaning:

God has saved

First Reference:

2 Kings 19:2

Last Reference:

Isaiah 39:8

Key References:

2 Kings 19:20–24; 20; Isaiah 1:1

Jacob

SON OF ISAAC AND FATHER
OF THE ISRAELITE TRIBES

After this, his brother came out, with his hand grasping Esau's heel;
so he was named Jacob. Isaac was sixty years old when
Rebekah gave birth to them.
GENESIS 25:26 NIV

It's not uncommon for parents to give their children names
that express the hopes they have for them or the attributes
they associate with them: Joy, Hope, Victor, Hunter, and so on.
So how about the idea of *deceiver*? That's exactly the sentiment
expressed by the name Jacob.

Jacob, also called Israel, was the son of Isaac and the father
of the twelve patriarchs of Israel. He and his older brother,
Esau, were twins—and when they were born, Jacob was grasping the heel of Esau (Genesis 25:26), so he was given the name
Jacob ("heel holder"). In ancient Israel, to "grasp the heel"
meant to deceive or supplant, which was somewhat fitting for
Jacob's personality throughout much of his life.

Some of the ways that Jacob deceived or supplanted others
include convincing Esau to trade his birthright for a bowl of stew
(Genesis 25:29–34), tricking Isaac to gain the blessing he wanted
to give Esau (Genesis 27), and fooling his uncle Laban to increase
his flocks (Genesis 30). Later, after Jacob wrestled with a man of
God at the Jabbok River, his name was appropriately changed to
Israel, meaning "one who strives with God" (Genesis 32).

One of Jacob's twelve sons was Joseph, who rose to a position of second in command of Egypt, and Jacob and his family moved to Egypt to live with him there. After Jacob had grown very old, he blessed his twelve sons and died (Genesis 37–50).

Related Information:
Once, even Jacob the Deceiver was deceived by his uncle Laban. Jacob had worked for seven years to pay the bride price for Rachel, but Laban gave Jacob Rachel's older sister, Leah, instead. Jacob had to work another seven years for Rachel (Genesis 29).

Meaning:
Supplanter

First Reference:
Genesis 25:26

Last Reference:
Hebrews 11:21

Key References:
Genesis 27:27–29, 39–40; 32:28–30

44

Jairus

Synagogue Official
Whose Daughter Died

Then a man named Jairus, a synagogue leader, came and fell at Jesus'
feet, pleading with him to come to his house because his only daughter,
a girl of about twelve, was dying.
Luke 8:41–42 NIV

It's the reason ambulances are allowed to run red lights and emergency rooms stand ready to deal with virtually any life-threatening situation: Life is fragile, and time is critical when emergencies arise. Surely this was what Jairus must have been thinking when he came to Jesus, fell at His feet, and pleaded for Him to come and heal his dying daughter (Luke 8:40–56). And if we find ourselves perplexed by Jesus as He took time to find out who touched His garment amid a great crowd, we are probably thinking the same thing about life.

But Jesus didn't see things that way. There is no mention of urgency in His pace, no mention of concern about whether they would reach the girl in time to help her. And even when someone informed Jesus along the way that Jairus's daughter had already died, no mention is made that Jesus expressed any despair. The Bible doesn't record Jairus's reaction, but he may have wondered whether Jesus really cared what happened to his daughter. But Jesus responded this way not because He was uncaring, but because He knew He had no reason to worry—His Father was in complete control of the situation (Luke 8:50).

When Jesus finally arrived at the house, He simply made His way to where the girl was, took her by the hand, and raised her to life again. Such is the power of God—and the reason that we, too, can always find great assurance and peace in Him.

Related Information:

Jairus was said to be a "ruler of the synagogue" (Luke 8:41 ESV), which probably meant that he was in charge of arranging the services for the local synagogue each Sabbath day. The book of Acts makes reference to two other people who were rulers of the synagogue (Acts 13:15; 18:8).

Meaning:
Enlightener

First Reference:
Mark 5:22

Last Reference:
Luke 8:41

JAMES

BROTHER OF JESUS AND LEADER OF JERUSALEM CHURCH

Then after three years, I [Paul] went up to Jerusalem to get acquainted with Cephas and stayed with him fifteen days. I saw none of the other apostles—only James, the Lord's brother.
GALATIANS 1:18–19 NIV

James, often called James the Just, seems to be an enigma in virtually every way. He is at the center of several controversies surrounding the history of the early church.

What is generally agreed upon about James is that he was the leader of the Jerusalem church, and he was in contact with such leaders as Peter, John, Barnabas, and Paul. At the first church council in Jerusalem, James was instrumental in forging the church's position regarding Gentiles and the law of Moses (Acts 15). Beyond this, it seems like everything else is in dispute.

Regarding his relationship to Jesus, there is debate whether he was Jesus' half brother, Jesus' stepbrother, Jesus' cousin, or something else.

Regarding his theology, James's emphasis on works rather than faith alone has led some to argue that he stands in opposition to Paul's emphasis on salvation by grace through faith—but others argue that the two positions complement and balance each other.

Regarding archaeological evidence of his existence, a controversy erupted in 2002 when a tomb purported to be his was made public, but later it was deemed to be a fake by the Israeli Antiquities Authority.

Despite all these controversies, however, James's letter to the scattered believers has always been a favorite due to its very practical wisdom and instruction. It is often referred to as the Proverbs of the New Testament.

Related Information:

According to the Jewish historian Josephus, the Sanhedrin charged James with breaking the law and stoned him to death around AD 62.

Meaning:

--

First Reference:

Matthew 13:55

Last Reference:

Jude 1:1

Key References:

Mark 6:3; 15:40; 1 Corinthians 15:7; Galatians 2:9

JEPhThah

JUDGE OF ISRAEL WHO
MADE A FOOLISH VOW

And Jephthah made a vow to the LORD: "If you give the Ammonites into my hands, whatever comes out of the door of my house to meet me when I return in triumph from the Ammonites will be the LORD's, and I will sacrifice it as a burnt offering."
JUDGES 11:30–31 NIV

In the book of Ecclesiastes, the teacher wisely instructed his listeners, "Do not be quick with your mouth, do not be hasty in your heart to utter anything before God. God is in heaven and you are on earth, so let your words be few" (Ecclesiastes 5:2 NIV). Unfortunately for Jephthah and his daughter, the teacher didn't write those words until long after this story in Judges.

Jephthah lived during the time of Israel's judges, an outcast among his own family because he was the son of a prostitute. Still, he had the opportunity to make a name for himself when the leaders of Israel needed help fighting the Ammonites, who were oppressing them. Jephthah agreed, but with the condition that he rule the people if he was victorious over the Ammonites. As he was preparing to battle the enemy—no doubt calculating the high stakes of the outcome—Jephthah made a rash vow to the Lord: he promised to sacrifice the first thing that came out of his house to greet him if he won.

Jephthah was indeed victorious over the Ammonites, but

when he returned home, he was shocked to find his daughter, rather than some chicken or goat, running out to greet him first. So Jephthah offered his daughter as a sacrifice (Judges 11).

Related Information:

In another battle against some of his fellow Israelites, Jephthah and his men capitalized on a pronunciation difference between the Ephraimites and the Gileadites. Whenever a person wanted to cross one of Jephthah's checkpoints, he would have to pronounce the word "Shibboleth." An Ephraimite could be detected immediately, because he would be unable to pronounce the *sh* sound and would pronounce the word as "Sibboleth."

Meaning:
He will open

First Reference:
Judges 11:1

Last Reference:
1 Samuel 12:11

Key References:
Judges 11:5–10, 29–30

JEREMIAH

PROPHET OF JUDAH

"Do not be afraid of them, for I am with you and will rescue you," declares the LORD. Then the LORD reached out his hand and touched my [Jeremiah's] mouth and said to me, "I have put my words in your mouth."
JEREMIAH 1:8–9 NIV

No one wants to be the one to pass on bad news, especially if the people you are speaking to don't really want to hear the truth. But this was the painful ministry that the prophet Jeremiah was called to even before he was born (Jeremiah 1:5).

Jeremiah was probably only about twenty years old when the Lord informed him of his special calling to prophesy against His people. At first Jeremiah was reluctant, but the Lord told him not to fear the people, for He would be with him (Jeremiah 1:17–19). Jeremiah began his ministry in the days of the godly king Josiah, but he would eventually witness the destruction of Jerusalem and the temple at the hands of the Babylonians. All the while, he faithfully warned the people of the impending consequences of their wickedness and idolatry.

Jeremiah was often perceived as a traitor for preaching his messages of doom. Once, some royal officials of Judah even put Jeremiah in an empty cistern until he was rescued by a Cushite named Ebed-Melek (Jeremiah 38).

After the Babylonians attacked Jerusalem and destroyed the temple, some fleeing Judeans took Jeremiah with them to Egypt, where he prophesied more messages of doom and probably spent the rest of his life.

Spiritual Insight:

Have you ever faced a situation where you had to warn others about the consequences of their actions? Even if the people you are speaking to become angry or threaten you with harm, you do not need to fear—the Lord is with you, just as He was with Jeremiah.

Meaning:
God will rise

First Reference:
2 Chronicles 35:25

Last Reference:
Daniel 9:2

Key References:
Jeremiah 1:1, 5; 20:1–6; 21:3–6; 35:8–17; 37:12–15; 38:6

48

JESUS

SON OF GOD

"For even the Son of Man did not come to be served,
but to serve, and to give his life as a ransom for many."
MARK 10:45 NIV

The list of paradoxes about Jesus seems endless—born to die, fully God and fully man, served others though He was King of kings, betrayed to death by a kiss—but perhaps the greatest paradox is also the most wonderful for us: He died so that we might receive life.

Even Jesus' beginnings are difficult to describe, because as the third person of the Trinity, He has always existed (see John 1:1–3; 8:58). In terms of His earthly life, however, Jesus was born to Mary and Joseph, who descended from King David himself (Matthew 1–2; Luke 2–3). Jesus grew up in the town of Nazareth and became a carpenter like Joseph (Matthew 13:55; Mark 6:3).

Jesus began His public ministry of teaching and healing around age thirty (Luke 3:23), and His ministry lasted about three years. At the end of His ministry, some jealous Jewish leaders, looking for a way to get rid of Him, accused Him of treason before the Roman governor for His claim to be the Messiah, the King of the Jews. The Romans crucified Jesus along with two bandits, and He was buried in a borrowed rock tomb (Matthew 26–27).

Three days later, God raised Jesus to life again, just as He had promised. Later Jesus ascended to heaven until the time comes for Him to return to take His followers with Him to heaven (Matthew 28; Luke 24:50–53).

Spiritual Insight:

To read the bare facts about Jesus' life and death can mislead us into seeing Him as another tragic victim of an evil world—but the truth is that the world was merely carrying out the plan of God for the salvation of His people (Acts 2). Through Jesus' death, the price for sin was paid, and we can be made right with God (Romans 5). Praise God for sending Jesus to bring us eternal life in Him!

Meaning:

Jehovah saved

First Reference:

Matthew 1:1

Last Reference:

Revelation 22:21

Key References:

Matthew 5–7; Mark 11:7–9; Luke 4:18; 24:28–32; John 1:1, 14; 3:3–21; 20:10–22; Revelation 17:14; 19:11–16; 21:1–3

49

JEZEBEL

WICKED WIFE OF KING AHAB OF ISRAEL

There was never anyone like Ahab, who sold himself to do evil in the eyes of the LORD, urged on by Jezebel his wife.
1 KINGS 21:25 NIV

If the Bible gave a list of the most wicked women in history, Jezebel would almost certainly be at the top. Her life was marked by evil through and through, both by her own acts and the deeds she encouraged her husband to commit.

Jezebel was the daughter of King Ethbaal of Sidon (1 Kings 16:31), and she married King Ahab of Israel, probably to seal a political alliance between the two powers. Ahab had already demonstrated a love of idolatry and evil, and his marriage to Jezebel only compounded his sin.

Jezebel began to kill off the Lord's prophets, but Ahab's servant Obadiah secretly hid one hundred of them in a cave to save them. She personally supported hundreds of priests of Baal and Asherah (1 Kings 18:19), so when Elijah had them killed at the foot of Mount Carmel, Jezebel tried to kill him, too (1 Kings 19:1–2). She also arranged for a man named Naboth to be killed so that Ahab could seize his vineyard for himself (1 Kings 21).

Jezebel's wickedness did not go unnoticed by the Lord, however. Elijah prophesied that one day her body would become like refuse and be eaten by dogs by the wall of the city of Jezreel. This prophecy eventually came true at the hand of a usurper named Jehu (2 Kings 9).

Related Information:

Jezebel's hometown of Sidon was located in Phoenicia, whose people were famous throughout the ancient world for their extensive maritime activity. They had established trading colonies as far away as Spain and North Africa and were widely regarded as skilled sailors.

Meaning:
Chaste

First Reference:
1 Kings 16:31

Last Reference:
Revelation 2:20

Key References:
1 Kings 18:13; 19:1–3; 21:8–16; 2 Kings 9:7–10

JOB

GOOD MAN WHO SUFFERED

*In the land of Uz there lived a man whose name was Job. This man
was blameless and upright; he feared God and shunned evil.*
JOB 1:1 NIV

Suffering the consequences of our wrong actions can be
painful, but it pales in comparison to the pain that we feel
when we suffer for no apparent reason of our own. That is why
Job's painful experiences move us so deeply.

Job was a very successful man, with seven sons, three
daughters, and a wealth of livestock. In fact, "he was the greatest man among all the people of the East" (Job 1:3 NIV). The
Bible also makes it clear that Job was a righteous man. In a single day, however, nearly all his earthly blessings were snatched
away: all his animals were either stolen or destroyed, and every
single one of his children died in a terrible tragedy. Yet "in all
this, Job did not sin by charging God with wrongdoing" (Job
1:22 NIV).

But Job's sufferings were not over yet. He himself was
stricken with terrible sores from head to toe, and even his own
wife prodded him to give up on God (Job 2). Finally, some of
Job's friends came to mourn with him; but in the end, each of
them spent great energy trying to convince Job that he had
caused his own suffering by some hidden sin.

In all this, God was holding Job up as an example of a truly
righteous man, someone who would remain faithful even when

undergoing terrible suffering. That does not mean that Job did not question what God was doing and express anger over his condition. When God finally did answer Job, however, He made it clear that His ways are far above human ways and cannot truly be understood by human beings.

Job humbly recognized his place before God, and God blessed him once again with even more children and livestock.

Related Information:

The book of Job is written in both poetry and prose. The prose sections include the introductory section (which sets the scene and informs the reader of the dialogue between God and Satan) and the conclusion (which describes Job's restoration and blessing). The rest of the book is written in Hebrew poetry.

Meaning:
Hated, persecuted

First Reference:
Job 1:1

Last Reference:
James 5:11

Key References:
Job 1:21; 9:1–3; 13:12, 15; 19:25–27; 38:1–3; 40:4–5; 42:1–17

51

JOCHEBED

MOTHER OF MOSES, AARON, AND MIRIAM

*The name of Amram's wife was Jochebed, daughter of Levi,
who was born to Levi in Egypt; and she bore to Amram:
Aaron, Moses, and their sister Miriam.*
NUMBERS 26:59 NRSV

Jochebed was a risk-taker. Although the Bible doesn't give us a detailed biography of Moses' mother, it does disclose the results of the courageous choices she made.

When the Egyptian Pharaoh ordered the death of all newborn Hebrew boys in order to slow the slaves' population growth, Jochebed took decisive action to protect the life of her tiny son. The risks she took on Moses' behalf often go unnoticed:

- Jochebed risked punishment by defying the king's orders and letting her son live.
- She secretly hid her newborn baby for three months (Exodus 2:2).
- She risked her child's life by placing the infant in a floating basket in the Nile. She could not have known if this daring action would result in the baby being lost downstream, being discovered and killed, being drowned, being eaten by Nile crocodiles, or being discovered and spared.
- She risked exposure by having Miriam, her daughter, watch the basket and then approach the Egyptian princess with an offer of aid.

Though bold, Jochebed's choices were not reckless. A descendant of Levi, she had faith that God could intervene and save the boy she viewed as "a fine baby" (Exodus 2:2 NRSV).

Spiritual Insight:

Faith can be risky. We don't know what other risks Jochebed may have taken and how those turned out, but we do know that in this case God fulfilled His plan for the Hebrew people because of the risks she took. Doing what is right isn't always easy, and it can often be accompanied by a fair amount of risk. But when faith-based risks and God's plan coincide, the results can change the world.

Meaning:
Jehovah gloried

First Reference:
Exodus 6:20

Last Reference:
Numbers 26:59

JOHN

APOSTLE

When Jesus saw his mother there, and the disciple whom he loved
standing nearby, he said to her, "Woman, here is your son."
JOHN 19:26 NIV

The disciple whom Jesus loved." What title could anyone possibly want more than this? This title was the distinct privilege of the apostle John, the writer of the Gospel and letters that bear his name (John 13:23; 19:26; 21:7, 20).

We first read about John when he is chosen along with his brother James to leave his profession as a fisherman and become one of Jesus' disciples. John and his brother must have been somewhat of a rowdy pair, because Jesus nicknamed them "Sons of Thunder" (Mark 3:17). Nevertheless, John held some special place in Jesus' heart, because he was included in Jesus' "inner circle" of followers (Mark 5:37; 9:2; 13:3; 14:33) and was specifically given the responsibility to take care of Jesus' mother as Jesus neared death (John 19:26–27).

Soon after Jesus' resurrection, John and Peter healed a crippled man and were thrown into prison for preaching in the name of Jesus (Acts 3–4). Later John and Peter were sent to Samaria to confirm the genuineness of some Samaritans' conversion to Christianity (Acts 8). Years later John apparently moved to Ephesus, where he established his ministry among the churches of western Asia Minor. Near the end of his life, John was exiled to the island of Patmos off the coast of Asia

Minor, and there he wrote the book of Revelation, a vision of the final days of the world.

Spiritual Insight:

While John's title as "the disciple whom Jesus loved" certainly sets him apart as one who enjoyed a special relationship with Jesus, all believers in a sense can also claim this privileged title, for we are all followers (disciples) whom Jesus loves.

Meaning:
--

First Reference:
Matthew 4:21

Last Reference:
Revelation 22:8

Key References:
Matthew 4:21–22; 17:1–3; Mark 10:35–37; John 13:23; 19:26; 20:1–2

JOHN THE BAPTIST

FORERUNNER OF JESUS

John replied in the words of Isaiah the prophet, "I am the voice of one calling in the wilderness, 'Make straight the way for the Lord.'"
JOHN 1:23 NIV

John the Baptist was a man who clearly understood his calling: He was to prepare the way for the Messiah. So when the time came for Jesus to begin His ministry, John willingly directed others to Him and allowed his own powerful ministry to take a backseat to Jesus.

John was Jesus' relative, and his own birth, like Jesus', was foretold by the angel Gabriel (Luke 1). John grew up to be a prophet, living in the desert and dressing in clothing similar to Elijah's (2 Kings 1:8; Matthew 3:4). He preached the message, "Repent, for the kingdom of heaven has come near"—the same message Jesus would later preach (Matthew 4:17 NIV) after John baptized Him. Jesus held John in very high esteem, declaring that no man has ever been greater than he (Matthew 11:11). John's ministry and his call for repentance were so widespread that years after his death he had followers as far away as Ephesus (Acts 19:1–5).

As great as John's ministry was, however, he always understood that his role was to point to One who was greater: Jesus. John knew that Jesus was so great in comparison to him that he was not even worthy to untie Jesus' sandals (Mark 1:7).

John met his death when he was thrown in prison for

speaking out against Herod Antipas's marriage to his brother's wife. Herod's wife eventually asked for John's head on a platter, and Herod ordered that it be done.

Spiritual Insight:

John modeled the attitude that all believers should follow as we point others to Jesus. We may be serving Christ in a way that is very powerful and beneficial to many people, but ultimately Jesus is greater than anything we are doing. The time may come for us to allow our ministry to be overshadowed or even replaced by other things Jesus is doing, and we should imitate John's example and willingly allow that to happen.

Meaning:
--

First Reference:
Matthew 3:1

Last Reference:
Acts 19:4

Key References:
Matthew 3:7–10; 11:2–4; 14:1–12;
Mark 1:6–8; Luke 1:5–20

JONAH

RELUCTANT PROPHET TO PEOPLE OF NINEVEH

[Jonah] prayed to the LORD, "Isn't this what I said, LORD,
when I was still at home? That is what I tried to forestall by
fleeing to Tarshish. I knew that you are a gracious and
compassionate God, slow to anger and abounding in love,
a God who relents from sending calamity."
JONAH 4:2 NIV

From movies to books to workplace spats, it seems that revenge is in and mercy is out. That was true for Jonah as well. Jonah was a prophet from Israel who was called by God to preach to the people of Nineveh—the capital city of the mighty Assyrian Empire. This great empire was threatening to swallow up tiny Israel and everyone in it, and Jonah was not pleased about his new assignment.

So instead of heading for Nineveh, Jonah hopped on a slow boat to Tarshish—which was located in the opposite direction. But God cared too much about both Jonah and the people of Nineveh to let him go without a fight. So the Lord sent a storm that led the other sailors to throw Jonah overboard—then He sent a fish to snatch Jonah from a watery grave. In God's grace, Jonah was given a second chance to go to Nineveh to call the people to repent—and this time Jonah took it.

For most people, that's where the story stops, but that's really only half the story. The people of Nineveh did repent, and God, in keeping with His character, relented from carrying out the destruction He had threatened for the city. Good news, right? Not for Jonah. He was actually *angry* at God for being compassionate and sparing the city!

Spiritual Insight:

How do you respond when you are threatened or even hurt by others? Do you seek revenge? Do you pray for God to do nasty things to your enemies? Jesus calls us to pray for our enemies (Matthew 5:43–47). Since we have been spared eternal punishment for our sins (Romans 6:23), how can we wish anything else for others?

Meaning:
A dove

First Reference:
2 Kings 14:25

Last Reference:
Jonah 4:9

Key References:
Jonah 1:10–15; 4:10–11

Jonathan

Son of Saul and Friend of David

And Jonathan made a covenant with David because he loved him
as himself. Jonathan took off the robe he was wearing and gave it to
David, along with his tunic, and even his sword, his bow and his belt.
1 Samuel 18:3–4 niv

In a world that typically looks out for number one, we are
amazed and even puzzled by people like Jonathan, King Saul's
oldest son. In contrast with his father's flawed character, Jonathan
repeatedly demonstrated himself to be brave, capable, and loyal.

We first read about Jonathan when he was leading a thousand Israelite warriors to attack the Philistines (1 Samuel 13).
He and his armor bearer risked their lives climbing a cliff to
attack the Philistines and sent them into a panic. Jonathan's
leadership qualities earned him the respect of his men, who
they refused to allow Saul to kill Jonathan for unwittingly
going against Saul's orders (1 Samuel 14).

Perhaps even more impressive than Jonathan's bravery is
his selfless loyalty to David. Jonathan was poised to become the
next king after his father, but David's own acts of bravery were
establishing him as a leader among the people (1 Samuel 17).
Jonathan could easily have seen David as a threat, but instead he
became friends with David and pledged enduring loyalty to him
and his descendants—even sealing his commitment by giving
him his own robe and weapons (1 Samuel 18:1–4). Later
he tipped David off to Saul's intent to harm him, and David

had to flee (1 Samuel 20).

Jonathan died with his father in battle against the Philistines, and David composed a lament on his behalf (1 Samuel 31:1–2; 2 Samuel 1).

Related Information:

David was true to the pledge that he and Jonathan made to each other and their descendants. Years after Saul and Jonathan died, David sought out one of Jonathan's sons, Mephibosheth, and granted him all the property of his grandfather Saul. David also allowed him to eat at his table like one of his own sons (2 Samuel 9).

Meaning:

Jehovah given

First Reference:

1 Samuel 13:2

Last Reference:

Jeremiah 38:26

Key References:

1 Samuel 14:6–15; 18:1–4; 20:1–23; 31:2

56

JOSEPH

FAVORITE SON OF JACOB

But Joseph said to [his brothers], "Don't be afraid. Am I in the place of God? You intended to harm me, but God intended it for good to accomplish what is now being done, the saving of many lives."
GENESIS 50:19–20 NIV

Joseph was no victim. Though the Bible recounts episode after episode of wrongs being done to him, Joseph knew—or perhaps learned—that ultimately God was in charge of everything, and He was working all things together for the good of His people.

Joseph was the eleventh and favorite son of Jacob, and his favored status earned him resentment from his brothers, who eventually sold him as a slave to some merchants traveling to Egypt (Genesis 37). Once there, Joseph was sold to a royal official named Potiphar, who quickly recognized and benefited from Joseph's administrative gifts. Later Potiphar's wife falsely accused Joseph of assaulting her, and he was thrown into prison (Genesis 39).

While in prison, Joseph demonstrated the ability to interpret dreams, and he was brought before Pharaoh to explain some troubling dreams. Joseph correctly foretold a great famine that was going to come upon the whole world, so Pharaoh elevated him to second in command of the kingdom. The famine drove Joseph's brothers to Egypt for food as well, and after a series of interactions with them, Joseph revealed his identity to them (Genesis 40–45).

Joseph's brothers feared that he would seek revenge on them for selling him into slavery, but Joseph recognized that God was orchestrating the events of his life for the good of His people—and that he should not assume the role of God and repay his brothers for their wrongs against him (Genesis 50).

Spiritual Insight:

When others commit wrongs against us and cause us hardship, it is understandable if we feel angry and desire that God bring justice to our situation. Ultimately, however, we should recognize that we are not really at their mercy but at the mercy of God, who loves us and is always working all things together for our good (Romans 8:28–29).

Meaning:
Let him add

First Reference:
Genesis 30:24

Last Reference:
Hebrews 11:22

Key References:
Genesis 37:3–8, 24–28; 41:14–40;
42:6–28; 44:16–34; 45:3–10

57

JOSEPh

EARTHLY FATHER OF JESUS

An angel of the Lord appeared to him in a dream and said, "Joseph
son of David, do not be afraid to take Mary home as your wife,
because what is conceived in her is from the Holy Spirit."
MATTHEW 1:20 NIV

Along with great pride, most new fathers feel some amount of anxiety over the new responsibilities they face. But no one has ever really understood the burden placed on Joseph's shoulders: raising the Son of God. Where's the manual for that one? Who would you ask for advice?

Even before Jesus was born, however, Joseph had faced a great deal, and his good character was already beginning to show. When he learned that his fiancée, Mary, was pregnant with a child that wasn't his, he mercifully planned to divorce her quietly and spare her public disgrace. Then an angel appeared to him in a dream and told him that he should marry her—because the baby was conceived by the Holy Spirit and would be the Savior of the world (Matthew 1:18–21).

When Mary gave birth to Jesus, Joseph watched, no doubt amazed, as people came from far and near to worship the baby as the divine King. Then an angel appeared to him again and warned him to take his family to Egypt to avoid being killed by King Herod. Later Joseph returned to his hometown of Nazareth, where he continued to raise Jesus, the Savior of the world (Matthew 2).

When Jesus was twelve, Joseph and Mary were reminded again of Jesus' true identity when they found Him in the temple astounding the teachers with His questions. Jesus reminded them that the temple was His true Father's house, so it should be no surprise that He would be there (Luke 2:40–52).

Related Information:

Joseph was apparently a carpenter by trade (Matthew 13:55), and he must have passed these skills on to Jesus as well, because Jesus is also referred to as a carpenter in one of the Gospels (Mark 6:3).

Meaning:
Let him add

First Reference:
Matthew 1:16

Last Reference:
John 6:42

Key References:
Matthew 1:18–25; Luke 2:4–7

Joshua

Hebrew Military Leader

*"But charge Joshua, and encourage and strengthen him,
for he shall go over at the head of this people, and he
shall put them in possession of the land that you shall see."*
Deuteronomy 3:28 esv

Moses led the people to the doorstep of the Promised Land,
but Joshua helped the people walk through the door to
conquer and settle the land. Though born a slave in Egypt,
Joshua became Moses' primary aide and assistant (Exodus
24:13). During four decades at Moses' side, Joshua served in a
variety of ways: He explored the Promised Land as one of the
original twelve spies—along with Caleb, giving the only favor-
able report. He led the people into their first successful military
battles (Exodus 17). And he joined Moses on the mountain of
God (Exodus 24:13). After Moses' death and the completion
of a forty-year apprenticeship, Joshua became the leader of the
Hebrew people (Joshua 1–4).

Joshua assumed command during a time of military conquest. Having commissioned Moses to lead the people out of
Egypt, God gave Joshua the job of leading them into Canaan.
Under Joshua's leadership the people conquered Jericho, Ai,
and the other people of the land (Joshua 12). After the dust of
battle settled, Joshua divided and assigned the land as instructed
by Moses (Joshua 13–19).

Even though Joshua's legacy primarily revolves around his

military exploits, each of his conquests is marked by his faith in God. Urging the people to remember the teachings of Moses, Joshua constantly reminded them of God's presence and plan. He entered into battle with a dependence on God's strength. He lived out the exhortation he received at the beginning of his days in leadership: "Have I not commanded you? Be strong and courageous. Do not be frightened, and do not be dismayed, for the LORD your God is with you wherever you go" (Joshua 1:9 ESV).

Did You Know?

The name *Jesus* is derived from *Joshua*. Just as Joshua brought God's people into a physical Promised Land, so Jesus brings God's people into a spiritual Promised Land. Read more on this comparison and theme in Hebrews 4.

Meaning:
Jehovah saved

First Reference:
Exodus 17:9

Last Reference:
1 Kings 16:34

Key References:
Numbers 14:6–7, 30; 27:18–23;
Joshua 6:2–21; 10:12–13; 13:1, 6; 24:15

59

Josiah

THE REFORMER KING

*Josiah removed all the detestable idols from all the territory belonging
to the Israelites, and he had all who were present in Israel serve
the LORD their God. As long as he lived, they did not fail to
follow the LORD, the God of their ancestors.*
2 CHRONICLES 34:33–34 NIV

Imagine if the Bible disappeared—lost to history, with no surviving copies to be found. How would you know how to relate
to God? How could you tell if you were obeying His will?

That was Judah's dilemma when Josiah took the throne
at the age of eight. The Book of the Law had not been seen
or read for generations—perhaps not since Hezekiah, the last
good king of Judah (and Josiah's great-grandfather). Since
then, Judah had sunk to new lows, particularly during the reign
of Manasseh, who sacrificed humans and defiled the Jewish
temple—only to be humiliated when the Assyrians took him
prisoner.

Josiah had reigned for eight years when he decided to turn
things around and follow God. Still a teenager, he implemented
top-down reforms with zeal, obliterating pagan worship sites
and repairing the temple. But with no Book of the Law to
guide him, how would Josiah know what else needed to be
done?

While cleaning the temple, a priest named Hilkiah redis-
covered the Book of the Law. It was brought to Josiah and read

aloud—but rather than celebrate, Josiah lamented. Its words were a painful reminder of how far the Israelites had wandered from God's ways. Even worse, the prophetess Huldah announced that it was too late for Judah to escape judgment. The only consolation for Josiah was that he would not live to see its demise.

This, however, did not discourage him from pursuing reform. He ordered the Book of the Law read aloud to the people, renewed the covenant with God, and reinstated the Jewish feast. Unfortunately, Josiah's untimely death in battle meant the throne passed to his son, Jehoahaz—who lasted just three months.

Spiritual Insight:

Josiah followed God, even though he knew his country was doomed. His legacy of faithfulness is recorded for all to read in the scriptures. Josiah's life serves as a reminder of the value of unwavering devotion to God, even when the whole world seems to be moving in the opposite direction.

Meaning:
Founded of God

First Reference:
1 Kings 13:2

Last Reference:
Zephaniah 1:1

Key References:
2 Kings 22:1–2, 10–13; 23:1–3, 5, 21, 29;
2 Chronicles 34:1–3, 31–33; 35:20–24

60

Judas Iscariot

BETRAYER OF CHRIST

Then Jesus replied, "Have I not chosen you, the Twelve?
Yet one of you is a devil!" (He meant Judas, the son of Simon Iscariot,
who, though one of the Twelve, was later to betray him.)
JOHN 6:70–71 NIV

Scholars have long debated the reason for Judas's betrayal of Jesus—suggesting as possible motives everything from greed to disillusionment.

Some believe Judas did it for the money. The blood payment, thirty pieces of silver, equaled four months' salary. According to John's Gospel, Judas was a thief who liked to "help himself" to money set aside to support Jesus' ministry (John 12:6 NIV).

Another theory notes that Judas was one of the only non-Galilean disciples. His surname, Iscariot, likely indicates his birthplace—Kerioth, a town in southern Judah. As an outsider, Judas may have felt alienated from the group.

Others insist that Judas was a Zealot, part of a Jewish guerrilla movement bent on driving out the Romans by any means necessary. As it became clear that Jesus had no intention of waging a war, Judas grew disillusioned or fearful (or both) and began looking for a way out.

A variant on this theory suggests that Judas didn't mean to betray Jesus at all—that Judas was merely trying to force His hand, convinced Jesus would give the call to arms once He was confronted in the garden of Gethsemane.

Still others chalk it up to demonic possession, noting—as Luke does—that "Satan entered Judas" shortly before the betrayal (Luke 22:3 NIV) and leaving it at that.

Whatever the real reason (or reasons), it is clear that Judas did not see the world as Jesus did. In one of the only stories to mention Judas outside of his betrayal, he scoffed at the so-called waste of expensive perfume by the woman from Bethany (see John 12:1–11). Jesus saw the woman's gift as an act of devotion, preparing Him for His impending death and burial. Judas only saw money being poured down the drain—money he wanted for himself. Judas demonstrated greed, hypocrisy, and an unwillingness to associate himself with Jesus' death—values that have no place in God's kingdom.

Did You Know?

The disciples' first order of business after Jesus' ascension was replacing Judas. In the book of Acts, Luke chose not to spare his readers the grisly details of Judas's suicide, noting that the betrayer's "body burst open and all his intestines spilled out" (Acts 1:18 NIV).

Meaning:
Celebrated

First Reference:
Matthew 10:4

Last Reference:
Acts 1:25

Key References:
Matthew 27:3–5; Mark 14:10; John 13:2, 26

Lazarus

Raised from the Dead

When he had said this, Jesus called in a loud voice,
"Lazarus, come out!"
John 11:43 NIV

azarus and Jesus were so close that names did not need to be mentioned when word reached Jesus that His friend was ill. He was simply told, "The one you love is sick" (John 11:3 NIV).

Lazarus and his sisters, Mary and Martha, probably belonged to a wealthy family, as evidenced by the expensive perfume Mary poured on Jesus' feet after He raised Lazarus from the dead. It is possible the three siblings supported Jesus' ministry financially.

In any case, a deep bond existed between Lazarus and Jesus—so much so that Jesus willingly risked His life returning to Judea in order to "wake him up" (John 11:11 NIV). By the time Jesus arrived, however, Lazarus was unquestionably dead. John notes that Lazarus had been in the grave four days, which was significant because of the widely held Jewish belief that the soul departed the body three days after death. In other words, people might have accepted the possibility that Lazarus could be raised within the first three days—that is, before he was truly, irreversibly dead, but any hope of resurrection evaporated after the fourth day.

Jesus, however, was undeterred.

Led to the tomb where Lazarus was buried, He became deeply troubled at the sight of Lazarus's sisters grieving—and almost certainly by His own grief as well. Jesus ordered Lazarus to come out of his tomb, and to the crowd's amazement, he obeyed.

No one knows how long Lazarus lived after being brought back to life, but this miracle set in motion the events that led to Jesus' own death and resurrection. Incensed at Jesus' growing popularity, the Pharisees decided the time had come to put Jesus to death.

Spiritual Insight:

One thing is known about Lazarus's postresurrection life: Like Jesus, he became the target of an assassination plot. As far as the religious leaders were concerned, a living and breathing Lazarus was almost as great a threat to their authority as the One who had raised him. Lazarus's story, then, is a picture of the cost of following Jesus. With new life comes new risk—and new opportunity to sacrifice all for Christ.

Meaning:
--

First Reference:
John 11:1

Last Reference:
John 12:17

Leah

Jacob's First Wife

When the Lord saw that Leah was unloved,
he opened her womb; but Rachel was barren.
Genesis 29:31 NRSV

It is generally not a good sign when a person's name means either "weary" or perhaps "wild cow." More than once, Leah found herself a pawn in someone else's scheme, unloved and unwanted. But God made her a pillar of His chosen people, the Hebrews.

Leah's misfortune began when her father, Laban, used her to trick Jacob. Jacob had grown smitten with Laban's younger and more beautiful daughter, Rachel, and agreed to work seven years in order to marry her. On the wedding night, Laban switched brides without Jacob realizing it until the following morning. When Jacob saw Leah—whom the Jewish historian Josephus described as "devoid of beauty"—he was furious. For the rest of his life, Jacob never loved Leah the way he loved Rachel.

In response, God blessed Leah, enabling her to bear six sons and a daughter while her sister, Rachel, remained almost completely barren. Fertility was seen as a sign of divine favor in the ancient world.

Still, Jacob remained indifferent toward Leah. Initially convinced that the birth of her sons would win Jacob's affection, Leah came to terms with her situation by the time Judah was born. She contented herself with being the recipient of God's favor instead.

Years later, as Jacob prepared to meet his estranged brother, Esau, Leah received another reminder of her status. Fearful that Esau would attack, Jacob arranged his family in reverse order of importance—sending the servants and their children first, Leah and her children second, and Rachel and her son, Joseph, last. Leah was at least more valuable to Jacob than his servants, but she was still clearly the second favorite.

God's favor, however, secured an important place for Leah in Israel's history. One of her sons, Levi, became the ancestor of the Jewish priesthood, while another, Judah, was the father of Israel's lone dynasty.

Did You Know?

Leah's name, along with Rachel's, was invoked in a blessing at the marriage of Ruth and Boaz—the great-grandparents of King David. The elders of Bethlehem prayed that God would make Ruth "like Rachel and Leah, who together built up the house of Israel" (Ruth 4:11 ESV).

Meaning:
Weary

First Reference:
Genesis 29:16

Last Reference:
Ruth 4:11

Key References:
Genesis 29:20–28, 31–35; 30:9, 17–21;
33:1–2; 34:1–2; 49:31

63

LOT'S WIFE

WIFE OF ABRAHAM'S NEPHEW

But Lot's wife looked back, and she became a pillar of salt.
GENESIS 19:26 NIV

Lot's wife garners only a single verse in all of scripture, but her actions and punishment raise some very significant questions. Did she look back longingly for what she was leaving? Or did she look back to see the punishment that was befalling those who did not escape Sodom?

Lot was the nephew of the patriarch Abraham, who accompanied him to Canaan. At some point in their time in Canaan, the two men decided to separate to avoid conflicts over land for their vast herds. Lot chose the lush valley of the Jordan River and Dead Sea, so he moved to Sodom, which was likely located along the eastern coast of the Dead Sea (Genesis 13).

Sodom was a wicked city, and eventually the Lord destroyed it by raining burning sulfur down on it. Before He did, however, He sent two angels to lead Lot's family to safety away from the city. While they were leaving the city, Lot's wife disobeyed the warning of the angels and looked back—and she was turned into a pillar of salt (Genesis 19:17, 26).

The Bible does not make it clear *why* she looked back, so we are left wondering exactly why she was punished. One thing is clear, though: When the Lord leads us away from sin and its consequences, there is nothing to be gained by looking back.

Related Information:

In the New Testament, Jesus tells His listeners to "remember Lot's wife" on the day when the Lord comes for His people (Luke 17:32 NIV). In that context, He seems to suggest that Lot's wife was looking back in longing for what she was leaving behind.

Meaning:

--

First Reference:

Genesis 19:26

Last Reference:

Luke 17:32

LUKE

PAUL'S TRAVELING COMPANION

*It seemed good to me also, having followed all things closely
for some time past, to write an orderly account for you,
most excellent Theophilus, that you may have certainty
concerning the things you have been taught.*
LUKE 1:3–4 ESV

Surprisingly little is known about the man who wrote a quarter of the New Testament. What is known, however, is that Luke brought his unique set of skills to bear—including his expertise as a physician and his keen eye for detail—in writing an account of the life of Jesus and the early church.

Luke was not an eyewitness to Jesus' ministry. At the beginning of his Gospel, he described himself as a researcher who "carefully investigated everything" (Luke 1:3 NIV). Of the four Gospels, Luke's has the most in common with classical Greek literature—its sophisticated style of writing reflects favorably on the author's education.

However, Luke was no ivory tower academic, writing about things from afar. Luke was friends with the apostle Paul. Beginning with Paul's second missionary journey, the two men became traveling companions. (Notice Luke's use of the pronoun "we" starting in Acts 16:10.) As such, Luke witnessed firsthand many of the incidents recorded in the book of Acts. He may well have suffered imprisonment and persecution alongside Paul. He was there with Paul when a ship bound for

Crete broke apart, nearly drowning everyone on board. Some believe he put his medical training to use at key moments, such as when Paul was bitten by a snake on the island of Malta.

Luke was part doctor, part historian, and part adventurer—but most of all, he was a dedicated, articulate, compelling advocate for the good news of Jesus Christ.

Did You Know?

Luke is probably the only Gentile author represented in the New Testament. Near the end of his letter to the Colossians, Paul included Luke in a list of Gentile companions who sent their greetings to the believers in Colosse (see Colossians 4:14).

Meaning:

--

First Reference:
Colossians 4:14

Last Reference:
2 Timothy 4:11

LyDia

FIRST BELIEVER FROM PAUL'S MINISTRY IN EUROPE

One of those listening was a woman from the city of Thyatira named Lydia, a dealer in purple cloth. She was a worshiper of God. The Lord opened her heart to respond to Paul's message.
ACTS 16:14 NIV

Lydia has the great distinction of being the first person in Europe to respond to Paul's presentation of the gospel.

Paul met Lydia in the city of Philippi while he was on his second missionary journey. He had just sailed from the city of Troas in Asia Minor to the port city of Neapolis, which is near Philippi in Macedonia (northern Greece). There must not have been very many Jews in Philippi, because Paul did not go to a synagogue on the Sabbath as he usually did. Instead, he went to a nearby riverbank, where any Jews who did live there would likely have met for prayer.

There he found several women, including Lydia, a "worshiper of God," which usually meant a Gentile convert to Judaism. She was actually from the city of Thyatira in Asia Minor and was likely wealthy, since she was a dealer in purple cloth. When Paul began to speak to the women about the gospel, Lydia responded, became a believer, and was baptized. Later she invited Paul and his companions to stay with her family. Still later, after Paul and Silas were released from prison, they returned to Lydia's house, encouraged the fledgling church that was started there, and then left to travel farther throughout Macedonia.

Related Information:

By the time of Paul, Philippi, which not large, was a significant Roman city—home to many retired Roman soldiers and granted exemption from most taxes.

Meaning:
--

First Reference:
Acts 16:14

Last Reference:
Acts 16:40

MALCHUS

CAIAPHAS'S SERVANT

"Put your sword back in its place," Jesus said to him, "for all who draw the sword will die by the sword."
MATTHEW 26:52 NIV

Malchus was a personal servant to Caiaphas, the high priest who led the conspiracy to have Jesus arrested and killed. Probably on Caiaphas's orders, Malchus accompanied Judas and the party seeking to arrest Jesus while He prayed in the garden of Gethsemane. As the situation threatened to explode into chaos, Malchus found himself very much in the wrong place at the wrong time.

Cornered, Jesus' disciples watched the horrifying scene unfold—one, however, decided to act. Peter unsheathed a sword and swung, severing Malchus's ear. It may have been the combination of instinct and adrenaline that drove Peter's hand. Or it may have been his failure to understand the true nature and purpose of Jesus' ministry. As Malchus writhed in pain, Jesus rebuked his attacker, warning Peter that "all who draw the sword will die by the sword" (Matthew 26:52).

Determined that no blood but His own be shed on His account, Jesus somehow managed to reach Malchus and heal his injury before being dragged away by the temple guard. Malchus, then, provided the object lesson in one last teaching to the disciples before Jesus' crucifixion—one final reminder that His kingdom would not come by force or be spread by the sword. What happened to Malchus after this incident—and whether he returned to his master, the man who plotted Jesus' murder—is unknown.

Did You Know?

While uncertain, the attack on Malchus may have had hidden significance. Assuming Malchus was a Levite, like his master and all who belonged to the priestly class, a defect like the loss of an ear would have rendered him unclean according to the law of Moses. Malchus would have been forbidden from going anywhere near the temple (see Leviticus 21). If this was the case, then Jesus not only restored Malchus's ear—He restored his livelihood.

Meaning:
--

Only Reference:
John 18:10

Martha

SISTER OF MARY AND LAZARUS

"Martha, Martha," the Lord answered, "you are worried and upset about many things, but few things are needed—or indeed only one. Mary has chosen what is better, and it will not be taken away from her."
LUKE 10:41–42 NIV

It seems like it's the same every holiday. We have good intentions of reflecting on the true meaning of the special day and focusing on Jesus, but inevitably we can never seem to fit this in amid all the busyness of preparing food or visiting family or buying gifts or whatever. We are too much like Martha and not enough like her sister, Mary.

Martha was the sister of Mary and Lazarus. The three of them lived near Jerusalem in a small village named Bethany. Because of their friendship with Jesus and their proximity to the holy city, Jesus seemed to regularly stay with them while he was in the area.

On one of these visits, Martha worked hard at serving Jesus and grew indignant when her sister, Mary, sat beside Jesus rather than help with the preparations. Jesus gently rebuked Martha instead, telling her that she was not choosing the most important thing: being in Jesus' presence.

Martha's busy nature can be seen again at a meal given in Jesus' honor in their home. Martha served while Lazarus reclined and ate with the other guests at the dinner. Mary later demonstrated her love for Jesus by pouring perfume on Jesus' feet and wiping His feet with her hair.

Spiritual Insight:

Though we should be careful not to write Martha off completely as someone consumed with daily chores and uninterested in spending time with Jesus, she does stand as a negative example to believers today. We should make sure that we are always keeping the main thing the main thing: spending time with Jesus and enjoying Him.

Meaning:
Mistress

First Reference:
Luke 10:38

Last Reference:
John 12:2

Key References:
Luke 10:38–42; John 11:1–44

MARY MAGDALENE

FOLLOWER OF JESUS

*Mary Magdalene went to the disciples with the news:
"I have seen the Lord!"*
JOHN 20:18 NIV

Mary Magdalene was one of Jesus' most devoted followers. She was among the last to leave His side after the Crucifixion and the first to witness His resurrection.

It's no wonder Mary was so devoted—Luke reports that Jesus delivered her from seven demons (Luke 8:2). In the ancient Jewish world, the number seven represented completion or totality. Mary's bondage was all-encompassing—then again, so was the healing that Jesus provided. From that day on, Mary Magdalene joined several other women who followed Jesus and supported His ministry financially.

The remaining biblical references to Mary Magdalene are all connected to the death and resurrection of Jesus. Long after many of Jesus' disciples had scattered, Mary and the other women lingered at the foot of the cross (see Matthew 27:56). As Jesus' body was laid in a borrowed tomb, Mary was there, watching the somber, lonely procession (see Matthew 27:61). And it was Mary Magdalene and "the other Mary" who ventured out from safety to anoint Jesus' broken body—only to find that the tomb was empty (see Matthew 28:1).

Mary had the honor of being the first person to bear witness to the resurrection. John provides an extended glimpse into Mary's encounter with the risen Christ. Her initial impression—that Jesus was the gardener—was not altogether mistaken. Jesus was, after all, the second Adam (see Romans 5:17), and the first Adam was originally a gardener. When Mary fully realized whom she was talking to, she was overcome with emotion. Jesus, however, encouraged her not to cling to Him—time was short and He had important work for her to do. Jesus entrusted Mary with the responsibility and privilege of being the first to spread the word that the Messiah had conquered death.

Did You Know?

Some of the church fathers believed that the sinful woman who anointed Jesus in Luke 7 and Mary Magdalene (introduced in Luke 8) were the same person—which gave rise to the popular myth that Mary was a prostitute. There is, however, nothing in scripture to support this. If Luke had wanted his readers to connect the woman in chapter 7 with Mary Magdalene (one of three women mentioned in Luke 8), he almost certainly would have mentioned her by name in the story of the sinful woman.

Meaning:
--

First Reference:
Matthew 27:56

Last Reference:
John 20:18

Key References:
Mark 15:40–41; 16:9; Luke 24:10–11; John 20:1–18

MARY

MOTHER OF JESUS

But the angel said to her, "Do not be afraid, Mary;
you have found favor with God. You will conceive and
give birth to a son, and you are to call him Jesus."
LUKE 1:30–31 NIV

Mary is, of course, best known as the virgin who gave birth to the Messiah—one of the most celebrated miracles in the Bible. But the New Testament also portrays Mary as a refreshingly human figure. In the Gospels, she is often characterized by her motherly concern for her son.

Twelve years after Jesus' miraculous birth, He accompanied His parents and their relatives and friends to Jerusalem for the Passover. When the time came to return home, Jesus lagged behind, wanting to spend more time among the rabbis in the temple. After three days of panicked searching, Mary and Joseph finally caught up with their son. The relief was obvious in Mary's words: "Son, why have you treated us like this? Your father and I have been anxiously searching for you" (Luke 2:48 NIV).

Years later, as Jesus began drawing large crowds—and as opposition started to form in some corners—Mary and her sons made a thirty-mile journey, intending to "take charge of him" (Mark 3:21 NIV). In all likelihood, Mary was concerned for Jesus' well-being; she simply wanted to protect her son from the ever-growing (and, no doubt, ever more demanding) crowds, not to mention the murmuring religious authorities who accused Jesus of being demon possessed.

The Gospel of John provides yet another fleeting glimpse of Mary—this time at the foot of her Son's cross. In the midst of His agony, Jesus spoke to His mother one last time. The sheer courage it must have taken to witness her Son's execution is astounding. One of Jesus' final acts before giving up His spirit was entrusting His mother to the care of His most beloved disciple, John (John 19:26–27). Even at the climax of redemptive history, Jesus paused to make sure the mother who had loved Him so well was cared for.

Spiritual Insight:

The Crucifixion was not the first time Mary demonstrated extraordinary courage. Submitting herself to God's plan meant risking years of scorn—and perhaps worse. In all likelihood, most would have scoffed at her account of the angelic visitation and miraculous conception. What's more, the Mosaic law stated that a betrothed virgin who slept with another man was to be stoned. Mary, however, demonstrated great trust in God's ability to protect her.

Meaning:

--

First Reference:

Matthew 1:16

Last Reference:

Acts 1:14

Key References:

Matthew 1:18–25; Luke 1:26–35; John 19:25

Matthew

Tax Collector Turned Disciple

*As Jesus went on from there, he saw a man named Matthew
sitting at the tax collector's booth. "Follow me," he told him,
and Matthew got up and followed him.*
Matthew 9:9 niv

Matthew sat at the crossroads of commerce. His tax collector's booth in Capernaum probably looked out on the Via Maris, one of the most important trading routes in the Roman Empire.

Local tax collectors were employed by the empire to keep Rome's coffers filled. They had a reputation for charging more than even Rome demanded and pocketing the extra—a habit that did not win many friends in occupied territories such as Galilee. In the ancient Jewish world, a tax collector's word was of no value in court, his presence was unwelcome at the synagogue, and even his own family might disown him.

Few would have approached Matthew's collection booth willingly—yet Jesus did. To some, it may seem strange that Matthew left behind a lucrative trade in order to wander the countryside with an itinerant preacher. Jesus, however, may have been one of the only people to offer Matthew an invitation of any kind. He may have been the first to look into Matthew's eyes—the eyes of one who, according to popular wisdom, should have been His enemy—and see a human being created in the image of God.

In that moment, Matthew left the crossroads of commerce to walk the crossroads of history. Not only did he accept Jesus' invitation—and extend one of his own, inviting Jesus to dinner—Matthew authored the Gospel that bears his name. Matthew wrote his account primarily for a Jewish audience—for the very people who had once despised him.

Spiritual Insight:

Matthew's dinner party caused great controversy among the religious leaders, mainly because the guest list contained so many tax collectors and "sinners"—in other words, people who deliberately violated God's law. The religious authorities were offended because fellowship with sinners was believed to contaminate—and in the ancient world, one of the most intimate forms of fellowship was sharing a meal. Jesus' response revealed that where others saw potential for contamination, Jesus saw an opportunity to bring healing and wholeness.

Meaning:

--

First Reference:

Matthew 9:9

Last Reference:

Acts 1:13

METHUSELAH

WORLD'S LONGEST-LIVING PERSON

Altogether, Methuselah lived a total of 969 years, and then he died.
GENESIS 5:27 NIV

There is no biblical reference to Methuselah outside of three genealogical records. Yet he is well known as the world's longest-living person, having survived, according to the Bible, for nearly a millennium.

The writer of Genesis recorded two family lines that descended from Adam and Eve. One was the family of Cain, the world's first murderer. The other was the family of Seth, to which Methuselah belonged. The two groups could not have been more different. Cain's family was industrious—playing musical instruments and working with metal—but it was also violent. Lamech, one of Cain's descendants, openly bragged about slaying two young men.

After chronicling Cain's descendants, the writer of Genesis notes that "at that time people began to call on the name of the LORD" (Genesis 4:26 NIV). With that, he launched into the account of the other family line—that of Seth. The most obvious characteristic of Seth's descendants was their propensity for long life spans. Five individuals mentioned, including Methuselah, exceeded nine hundred years. More important, however, this was the family that called upon God. Methuselah's father, Enoch, was the first man said to have "walked with God" (see Genesis 5:24 NASB). Methuselah's son, Lamech (no connection to the descendant of Cain), recognized God's role in their lives. And Methuselah's grandson Noah was found to be "blameless among the people of his time" (Genesis 6:9 NIV).

Perhaps even more remarkable than his age was the family to which Methuselah belonged—and their willingness to "call on the name of the LORD."

Did You Know?

Though Methuselah was history's longest-living person, the Bible records that he died the same year as the great flood of Noah's day. The Bible doesn't record if God graciously allowed him to die before the flood or if he was one of the wicked people who perished in the flood. No matter the final outcome of his life, Luke 3 records that Methuselah was one of the ancestors of Jesus Christ.

Meaning:
Man of a dart

First Reference:
Genesis 5:21

Last Reference:
1 Chronicles 1:3

MOSES

GREATEST HEBREW PROPHET

Now the man Moses was very humble, more than
any man who was on the face of the earth.
NUMBERS 12:3 NASB

Arguably Israel's greatest prophet, Moses left behind one of the strongest legacies in the Bible. As God's anointed leader, he led the people from Egypt to the Promised Land, appointed priests and judges, created a place of worship, delivered God's law, wrote the first five books of the Bible, and frequently interceded on behalf of the people. With this exceptional résumé, it's easy to envy a character like Moses. Who wouldn't want to accomplish so much?

For Moses, though, the road to each accomplishment included a great many difficult and rocky places as it twisted and turned. After becoming a fugitive from Pharaoh's court, Moses scratched out a living in the desert of Midian as a shepherd for forty years (Exodus 3). Once commissioned by God, Moses then risked his life by bringing bad news and judgment to Pharaoh (Exodus 4–12). And though God gave him the task of confronting Pharaoh, Moses lacked natural speaking ability and needed to rely on his brother, Aaron, to be his mouthpiece (see Exodus 4:10).

Securing the freedom of the Hebrew people led to more difficulty for Moses. Instead of being heralded as a hero, he became the object of the Israelites' complaints and rebellion (see examples in Exodus 15–17; Numbers 14, 16).

In spite of all his illustrious achievements as God's ap-pointed leader, Moses was not perfect. As a consequence for Moses' disobedience (Numbers 20), God did not allow him to cross into the land. Instead, God graciously allowed Moses to view the Promised Land that God had reserved for His people (Deuteronomy 34).

Related Information:

Moses' life illustrated that the price of leadership is often lone-liness. During the difficult times of leading the people through the wilderness, Moses faced opposition from those who should have been his closest allies. Leadership is difficult and lonely work. What leaders need to experience your support?

Meaning:
Drawing out (of the water), rescued

First Reference:
Exodus 2:10

Last Reference:
Revelation 15:3

Key References:
Exodus 3:2–18; 11:4–10; 12:29–30;
14:21–27; 20:1–17; Deuteronomy 34:5

Naaman

Syrian Army Commander

Now Naaman was commander of the army of the king of Aram. . . .
He was a valiant soldier, but he had leprosy.
2 Kings 5:1 niv

Naaman was an unlikely candidate for healing by a prophet from Israel. After all, he commanded the army of Aram (present-day Syria), one of Israel's adversaries.

Unfortunately, Naaman's reputation for valor was not enough to protect him from one of the most shameful diseases the ancient world knew: leprosy. Ironically, though, it was one of Naaman's prisoners of war who pointed the way to his eventual cure—a young Jewish servant girl suggested that Naaman visit the prophet Elisha.

Naaman sought the blessing of his master, the king of Aram, who sent a hefty payment to Israel's king in order to procure Elisha's services. Naaman and his master seemed unaware that Israel's prophets answered not to human authorities, but to God alone. At first, the bribe had the opposite of the intended effect, alarming the Israelite king, who suspected the Arameans of trying to pick another fight. But Elisha intervened, sensing an opportunity to demonstrate the superiority of the one true God—both to Naaman and to Israel's own unbelieving king.

Elisha staged his encounter with Naaman to leave no doubt as to who was responsible for the miraculous healing that took place. By refusing to meet Naaman face-to-face, Elisha made him realize that healing came from God, not from the superstitious incantations of a human prophet (see 2 Kings 5:11). By demanding that Naaman wash in the Jordan River—instead of allowing him to wash in waters belonging to Aram and to Aram's gods—Elisha asserted the supremacy of Israel's God over Aramean idols.

The carefully orchestrated episode left its mark on Naaman, who declared afterward, "Now I know that there is no God in all the world except in Israel" (2 Kings 5:15 NIV). The irony of the story is that a pagan warrior's eyes were opened to what so few in Israel were able to see.

Spiritual Insight:

Jesus mentioned Naaman as proof that ethnic or religious heritage does not entitle someone to God's favor. He noted that none of Israel's own lepers were healed in Elisha's time, but only Naaman (see Luke 4:24–27). Later Jesus commanded His followers to take the gospel to all nations, proving once more that God's love knows no geopolitical boundaries.

Meaning:
Pleasantness

First Reference:
2 Kings 5:1

Last Reference:
Luke 4:27

NaThaN

PROPHET TO KING DAVID

[David] said to Nathan the prophet, "Here I am, living in
a house of cedar, while the ark of God remains in a tent."
2 SAMUEL 7:2 NIV

Nathan was to David what Samuel was to Saul: a constant prophetic reminder that Israel's king was answerable to God. The only difference was that David actually listened to Nathan.

Nathan was present in three episodes of David's story. While his recorded appearances were few and far between, they suggested a closeness that existed between David and his trusted prophet. On the first occasion, David confided in Nathan his desire to build a permanent house for God to replace the portable tabernacle that had been used since the Israelites left Egypt. Nathan delivered God's answer—a refusal mixed with profound blessing. While God would not allow David to build Him a temple (that responsibility fell to his successor, Solomon), He promised to bless David with rest from his enemies and an everlasting dynasty (see 2 Samuel 7:1–17).

Sometime later, Nathan brought God's word to David once again—though under very different circumstances. David had seduced Bathsheba and arranged her husband's murder so he could take her as his own wife. Such behavior by the monarch would have been tolerated in almost any other kingdom—but not in Israel. Nathan confronted David, using the first parable recorded in the Bible to compare David to a rich man who stole a poor man's only lamb. David acknowledged his sin, but the damage was done. Nathan foretold that David and Bathsheba's first son would die—and that David and his heirs would forever be plagued by violence (see 2 Samuel 12).

In the final episode involving Nathan, the aging prophet worked to install one of David and Bathsheba's surviving sons, Solomon, on Israel's throne. God's favor had been with Solomon from birth (see 2 Samuel 12:24–25), so when another of David's sons conspired to take the throne, Nathan acted quickly—demonstrating shrewd political skills to match his prophetic wisdom. Together with Bathsheba, he convinced the dying King David to name Solomon heir to the throne.

Spiritual Insight:

Nathan's story proves that even prophets get it wrong sometimes—namely, when they don't wait for God's direction. After David shared his desire to build God's temple, Nathan approved the idea without hesitation. However, when God spoke to Nathan, revealing a different plan, the prophet returned to his king—this time with the correct advice.

Meaning:
Given

First Reference:
2 Samuel 7:2

Last Reference:
Psalm 51 title

Key References:
2 Samuel 7:3–12; 12:1–15; 1 Kings 1:11–14, 23–27

NEBUCHADNEZZAR,
KING OF BABYLON

"Now I will give all your countries into the hands
of my servant Nebuchadnezzar king of Babylon;
I will make even the wild animals subject to him."
JEREMIAH 27:6 NIV

No pagan ruler played a more prominent role in the biblical drama than King Nebuchadnezzar of Babylon. Nebuchadnezzar's exploits are well documented in both scripture and extrabiblical sources.

After a successful career commanding the Babylonian army, Nebuchadnezzar inherited his father's throne near the end of the seventh century BC. He reigned more than four decades.

Among his many conquests, Nebuchadnezzar made numerous incursions into Jewish territory. Initially, Nebuchadnezzar allowed Judah's kings to remain on the throne, so long as they kept up their tribute payments. The first of these kings, Jehoiakim, rebelled, switching loyalties from Babylon to Egypt. In retaliation, Nebuchadnezzar removed Jehoiakim from the throne and plundered the temple. Jehoiakim's successors, Jehoiachin and Zedekiah, fared no better. Finally, in 586 BC, Nebuchadnezzar razed Jerusalem, destroyed the temple, and carried the surviving inhabitants into exile. The kingdom of Judah was defeated.

For all his pomp and power, though, Nebuchadnezzar was nothing more than God's instrument. The prophet Jeremiah revealed that it was God who gave Judah into Nebuchadnezzar's hands (see Jeremiah 21:7). God was responsible for his victories over Tyre and Egypt (see Ezekiel 29:17–20).

Once, in response to Daniel's successful interpretation of a dream, the Babylonian king had acknowledged the supremacy of Israel's God (see Daniel 2:46–47). Soon, however, Nebuchadnezzar forgot and attributed his successes to his own "mighty power" (Daniel 4:30 NIV). In response, God afflicted Nebuchadnezzar with temporary insanity—as He had promised earlier. Once his sanity was restored, Nebuchadnezzar acknowledged the supremacy of the Lord once more. "His dominion," Nebuchadnezzar declared, "is an eternal dominion" (Daniel 4:34 NIV).

Did You Know?

Nebuchadnezzar is a rare, pagan contributor to the Bible. The fourth chapter of Daniel is attributed to the Babylonian ruler. Nebuchadnezzar's adulation of the one true God seems to have represented something less than true conversion, as he alluded to Marduk (also known as Bel, for whom Daniel was renamed Belteshazzar) as "my god" (see Daniel 4:8 NIV).

Meaning:
--

First Reference:
2 Kings 24:1

Last Reference:
Daniel 5:18

Key References:
2 Kings 24:1, 10, 12–14; 25:1, 6–7, 9–10;
Daniel 2:28–48; 3:13–30; 4:25–36

76

NICODEMUS

RELIGIOUS LEADER TAUGHT BY JESUS

"How can someone be born when they are old?" Nicodemus asked. "Surely they cannot enter a second time into their mother's womb to be born!"
JOHN 3:4 NIV

Nicodemus's faith did not appear in a moment of sudden illumination. Rather, it seems to have emerged gradually.

The Bible captures just three episodes from Nicodemus's life—all of them recorded in the book of John. In the first scene, Nicodemus sought an audience with Jesus, hoping to hear more from the popular rabbi. The nighttime setting has led many to conclude that Nicodemus feared the consequences of being seen publicly with the controversial Jesus. In His encounter with Nicodemus, Jesus told the inquisitive Pharisee that no one could experience God's kingdom without being reborn. Nicodemus, unable to distinguish between "earthly things" and "heavenly things" (see John 3:12 NIV), received a mild rebuke, accompanied by further explanation. It was to Nicodemus that Jesus revealed that faith in God's Son leads to eternal life.

John does not indicate whether Nicodemus walked away from the conversation having put his faith in Jesus, but the other two episodes featuring the religious leader are revealing. As the conspiracy against Jesus developed, some of the religious leaders rebuked the temple guards for not arresting Jesus when they had the chance. In response, the guards came to Jesus' defense, to which the Pharisees retorted that since no religious leader had put his faith in Jesus, neither should the guards. Apparently contradicting this claim, Nicodemus spoke up, challenging his colleagues for condemning Jesus without a hearing.

Once more, however, Nicodemus disappeared from the scene as quickly as he had appeared. He did not reemerge until the death of Jesus, when he, along with Joseph of Arimathea, took Jesus' body from the cross and buried it in an unused tomb—one final tribute to the Messiah who had once shared with him the secret of eternal life.

Spiritual Insight:

The phrase Jesus used to describe spiritual rebirth to Nicodemus can be translated "born again" or "born from above" (see John 3:3, 7 NIV). Either way, it describes a phenomenon that human beings are incapable of bringing about by their own will—we are wholly dependent on the grace of God.

Meaning:
Victorious among his people

First Reference:
John 3:1

Last Reference:
John 19:39

Noah

BUILDER OF THE ARK

By faith Noah, when warned about things not yet seen,
in holy fear built an ark to save his family.
HEBREWS 11:7 NIV

The unknown writer of Hebrews described Noah as a precursor of the kind of faith it would take to follow Christ. Noah's story was also a foreshadowing of the kind of redemption that God would provide for His people.

Noah lived during a time of rapidly escalating depravity. During this time, according to the author of Genesis, "every inclination" of the human heart had turned evil—much to God's anguish (see Genesis 6:5–6 NIV). As a "righteous man," Noah stood in marked contrast from the rest of civilization. Noah's righteousness was not superficial, yet it consisted of just one thing: Noah "walked with God" (see Genesis 6:9 NASB) while the rest of humanity walked in the other direction.

In Genesis, two descriptions of humanity's wickedness bookend the account of Noah's righteousness, evoking the impression that God's lone worshipper was in danger of drowning amid a sea of wickedness. God, however, had other plans—intending to drown humanity's wickedness in a sea of judgment, sparing only Noah and his family.

The details concerning Noah, the ark he built, and the flood that ensued are well-known. Acting on nothing but faith, Noah built the ark to God's exact specifications. Twice the writer noted that Noah did "all" or "everything" just as God commanded (see Genesis 6:22; 7:5 NIV).

As for the ark that Noah built, the Hebrew word is unique, used in Noah's story and in just one other place: the tale of the baby Moses being placed in a basket so he could escape Pharaoh's infanticide (see Exodus 2:3). Noah and his ark—and the deliverance it represented for those who follow God—anticipated the story of Moses and Israel's miraculous deliverance from the Egyptians. Also, according to the author of Hebrews, Noah's faith provided a model that all believes should follow in their devotion to Christ.

Meaning:
Rest

First Reference:
Genesis 5:29

Last Reference:
2 Peter 2:5

Key References:
Genesis 6:8–9, 14–16; 7:2–5, 24; 8:6–12, 20; 9:11–17

78

ONESIMUS

A RUNAWAY SLAVE WHO GAINED A NEW MASTER

I [Paul] appeal to you [Philemon] for my son Onesimus, who became
my son while I was in chains. Formerly he was useless to you,
but now he has become useful both to you and to me.
PHILEMON 1:10–11 NIV

As songwriter Bob Dylan put it, "You're gonna have to serve somebody." If Onesimus had lived in our day, he couldn't have agreed more.

Onesimus, a slave of a Colossian believer named Philemon, had run away from his master and somehow ended up meeting Paul. In an amazing display of the power of the gospel to change lives, Onesimus apparently became a believer and agreed to return to Philemon to face whatever consequences awaited him. At the same time, Paul sent a letter (now known as the New Testament book of Philemon) with him telling Philemon of how useful Onesimus, whose name means "useful," had become to him. In the letter, Paul urged Philemon to welcome Onesimus back as a brother rather than a slave. Paul even asked Philemon to charge to him any debt incurred by Onesimus, although Paul was quick to point out that Philemon owed his very self to Paul—most likely meaning that Paul had led Philemon to Christ.

And just in case Philemon needed some extra encouragement, Paul asked him to prepare a guest room in case he happened to stop as he passed through Colosse! Surely the thought of physically looking Paul in the eye was all the motivation he needed to do the right thing.

Spiritual Insight:

The question remains: Who are you going to serve? If you had asked Onesimus before he became a believer, he may have bitterly answered, "Philemon," or perhaps after he fled, "No one but myself." But in the end, we all serve somebody else—either the Lord or the devil. After Onesimus became a believer, he went back to Philemon perhaps expecting to return to a life of servitude, but really he was serving the Lord. Who are you going to serve?

Meaning:
Profitable

First Reference:
Colossians 4:9

Last Reference:
Philemon 1:10

Paul

Apostle to the Gentiles

I have become all things to all people so that by all possible
means I might save some. I do all this for the sake
of the gospel, that I may share in its blessings.
1 Corinthians 9:22–23 niv

The apostle Paul, the New Testament figure second only to Jesus in prominence, was a man of single-minded devotion. His mission to bring the gospel to the Gentile world filled him with an unrelenting fervor that carried him across the Roman Empire. In retrospect, Paul's background made him the perfect choice for this God-ordained mission.

Paul was born in the city of Tarsus (located in present-day Turkey), which was cosmopolitan and diverse; it was one of the leading university cities of its day. There Paul would have encountered all kinds of religious, cultural, and philosophical expressions.

But Paul was also devoted to the faith of his ancestors. He studied under Gamaliel, grandson of Hillel, the most famous rabbi of his day. As an adult, Paul bore all the markings of a rabbi. He even counted himself among the Pharisees.

Given his background, perhaps it is no surprise that God chose Paul to "carry my name before the Gentiles and kings" (Acts 9:15 esv). With one foot in the Jewish world and the other in the culture of the Gentiles, Paul was ideally suited to take the gospel from one to the other. His status as a Roman citizen—which suggests he belonged to the aristocracy—gave him enormous freedom as he traveled the empire. Paul used his citizenship not for his own gain, but to gain an audience with Caesar—knowing full well that to appeal to the Roman emperor (as only a Roman citizen could) was to put his very life at risk (see Acts 25:11). Paul's fate is not known. However, it is believed he gained his audience before Caesar—the dangerous Emperor Nero, to be precise—where he may well have become a martyr for the faith.

Spiritual Insight:

Despite his justifiably revered status in church history, Paul comes across as a refreshingly human figure. He was passionate—capable of great fits of emotion. The book of Acts even records Paul's falling out with his colleague Barnabas (Acts 15:36–41). Paul knew that he was just a sinner—in his mind, "the worst of sinners" (1 Timothy 1:16 NIV)—who had been saved by God's immeasurable grace.

Meaning:
Little

First Reference:
Acts 13:9

Last Reference:
2 Peter 3:15

Key References:
Acts 15:1–21; 17:22–33; 21:27–35; 25:8; 28:30–31

80

PETER

APOSTLE OF JESUS

But Peter declared, "Even if I have to die with you, I will never disown you." And all the other disciples said the same.
MATTHEW 26:35 NIV

Peter is one of the most passionate, impetuous, and volatile characters in the Bible. As such, he was simultaneously capable of great triumph and enormous failure. Peter's boundless enthusiasm was exceeded only by his love for his Master, Jesus.

Peter's original name was Simon. However, Jesus liked to call him Cephas, an Aramaic word meaning "rock" or "stone," which translated into Greek as "Peter." During the course of Jesus' ministry, Peter emerged as the natural leader among the disciples.

However, standing a head above the other disciples simply meant that Peter had further to fall—and he did. Immediately after his famous confession—which Jesus revealed was a result of divine enlightenment (see Matthew 16:17)—Peter proved equally adept at getting things wrong, contradicting Jesus' prediction of His own death (Matthew 16:22). Later, Peter confidently swore that he would stand with Jesus to the bitter end—that he would die with Jesus if the need arose. Not for the first time, though, Peter had misunderstood the fundamental nature of Jesus' ministry. When guards came to arrest Jesus, Peter reached for his sword and attacked the servant of the high priest. Peter believed the time had come to fight, not realizing that Jesus' mission was to lay down His life. Most famously, Peter wound up disowning his Master three times, much to his own dismay.

Despite all this, Jesus never gave up on Peter. According to Mark's Gospel, the angel at the tomb mentioned Peter by name when he told the women to share the news of Jesus' resurrection. Also, John recorded a particularly touching postresurrection scene in which Jesus restored Peter, entrusting to him the vital task of shepherding the early church.

Did You Know?

According to tradition, Peter was crucified for his faith. Some interpreters read Jesus' statement in John 21:18 NIV ("When you are old you will stretch out your hands, and someone else will dress you and lead you where you do not want to go") as a prediction of his martyrdom. Legend says that Peter requested to be crucified upside down because he did not consider himself worthy of being killed in the same manner as Jesus.

Meaning:
A piece of rock

First Reference:
Matthew 4:18

Last Reference:
2 Peter 1:1

Key References:
Matthew 14:28–33; 16:16; 17:1–8; John 18:10; 20:1–7; 21:15–19; Acts 2:14–41; 3:1–8; 4:13–20; 10:1–11:18

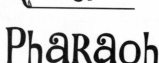

81

Pharaoh

King with a Hard Heart

But when Pharaoh saw that there was a respite, he hardened his heart and would not listen to them, as the LORD had said.
EXODUS 8:15 ESV

Pharaoh's determination to maintain power caused him to discount the obvious hand of God. Although the Bible doesn't record the name of this pharaoh (many scholars think it may have been Menephtah, son of Ramses II), it does tell of his ill-fated resolve.

As king of Egypt, Pharaoh struggled to maintain the power and order of the land. The vast Hebrew population provided a significant labor source and played an important role in Egypt's economy. As slaves, they helped build the infrastructure of the land—creating construction supplies and buildings (Exodus 5). If Pharaoh had yielded to Moses' demands, it would have dealt a blow to the kingdom, the economy, and his personal prestige.

Through Moses and Aaron, God inflicted Egypt with ten plagues designed to induce Pharaoh to release the Hebrew people and send them on their way to the Promised Land (Exodus 7–12). While many of the plagues initially motivated Pharaoh to release God's people, he changed his mind and held on to the people as soon as God removed the pain of the plague from the land. These plagues included turning the water into blood, infestations of frogs, lice, flies, and the death of cattle. They also included the infliction of boils, hail, locusts, and darkness.

Despite his grasping for power and his efforts to hold his kingdom's economy together, Pharaoh finally relented when the plagues became personal. The tenth plague (the killing of the firstborn son) directly affected Pharaoh's life and succession plan. Seeing his own dead son finally persuaded the king to release the people.

Spiritual Insight:

Pharaoh's stubbornness is no different than that of many in the world today. When they read of supernatural events in the Bible or hear of answered prayer, they explain away God's hand and continue to ignore the reality of God. Be careful that you don't dismiss your own blessings as good fortune or the mere fruits of your own hard work. Thank God for the times He answers your prayers.

Meaning:

--

First Reference:
Genesis 12:15

Last Reference:
Hebrews 11:24

Philip

Evangelist

Philip went down to a city in Samaria and proclaimed the Messiah there. When the crowds heard Philip and saw the signs he performed, they all paid close attention to what he said.
Acts 8:5–6 NIV

In His great commission to the disciples, Jesus revealed that His gospel was to smash all ethnic, national, and cultural barriers. Philip the evangelist embraced the inclusive nature of the gospel with inspiring zeal.

Philip was first mentioned as one of seven men chosen by the apostles to care for the widows who belonged to the Jerusalem church. Even this seemingly small service was a barrier-breaking act—Philip and his colleagues were responsible for making sure that the widows were treated equally, regardless of whether they were Hellenistic (Greek) or Hebraic Jews.

Later, when Saul's persecution scattered the church of Jerusalem, Philip seized the opportunity to go to Samaria. By extending the good news of Jesus, the Jewish Messiah, to the Samaritans, Philip shattered another centuries-old barrier.

The great evangelist was not finished with his barrier-breaking career, either. Having been directed by an angel, Philip journeyed from Jerusalem to Gaza, meeting an Ethiopian eunuch along the way. This man had two strikes against him. First, he was not Jewish (not even part Jewish, as the Samaritans were). Second, as a eunuch, Jewish law regarded him as ritually unclean—he was, in effect, "damaged goods." Yet Philip did not hesitate to sit with the eunuch and explain the gospel to him. The real test, however, came when the eunuch asked to be baptized. By agreeing to perform the ancient purification ritual, Philip acknowledged that in God's eyes, the eunuch was clean, pure, and whole.

Philip's life became the first of many signs that the good news of Jesus is for all people.

Did You Know?

The name Philip means "one who loves horses" in Greek. In the case of Philip the evangelist, this turned out to be an appropriate name, since he had to run up to a horse-drawn chariot in order to engage the Ethiopian eunuch in conversation! (See Acts 8.)

Meaning:
Fond of horses

First Reference:
Acts 6:5

Last Reference:
Acts 21:8

Key References:
Acts 8:5–8, 26–39

PONTIUS PILATE

PROCURATOR OF JUDEA

When Pilate saw that he was getting nowhere, but that instead an uproar was starting, he took water and washed his hands in front of the crowd. "I am innocent of this man's blood," he said.
MATTHEW 27:24 NIV

Pontius Pilate represented everything the Jewish leaders hated about Rome—its dominance, its oppression, and its idolatry. Yet when it came to the conspiracy to kill Jesus, the religious leaders were powerless to do anything without Pilate.

Ancient historians did not judge Pilate kindly. They saw an arrogant man who despised those he governed. Josephus noted that Pilate once tried to set up the Roman standards in the holy city of Jerusalem. Such graven images of the emperor—who claimed to be a god—were bad enough, but to have them so near the temple was an unbearable insult.

Later Pilate plundered the temple coffers to finance an aqueduct—once again infuriating the Jews. This time he had soldiers disguise themselves and mingle among the protesters gathered in Jerusalem, killing many. (Some believe this is the event Jesus mentioned in Luke 13:1–2.)

During the trial and execution of Jesus, Pilate demonstrated his disdain for the Jewish leaders—at one point deliberately provoking them by crucifying Jesus under a sign that read, THE KING OF THE JEWS. While the Roman procurator seemed in no hurry to condemn Jesus to death, his reluctance probably had less to do with any prevailing sense of justice (such a concept seemed utterly foreign to Pilate) and more to do with his desire for damage control. Pilate's subjects had already complained once to Rome about his oppressive rule. He didn't need another mark on his record, particularly at such a volatile time like the Jewish Passover festival.

Ultimately, Pilate's brutality proved his undoing when he was dismissed from office for slaughtering a number of Samaritans at Mount Gerizim around AD 37.

Spiritual Insight:

When Pilate asked Jesus if He was a king, Jesus famously responded, "My kingdom is not of this world" (John 18:36 NIV). Jesus did not deny Pilate's authority—instead, He masterfully subverted it, refusing to play by Pilate's rules. Pilate only knew how to command by the sword. In contrast, Jesus declared that His true followers, whose allegiance belonged to a higher authority, would not fight as Rome fought.

Meaning:
Close pressed

First Reference:
Matthew 27:2

Last Reference:
1 Timothy 6:13

Key References:
Matthew 27:11–26; Luke 23:6–11; John 18:29–19:15

QUEEN OF SHEBA

SOLOMON'S ROYAL VISITOR

Arriving at Jerusalem with a very great caravan—with camels carrying spices, large quantities of gold, and precious stones—she came to Solomon and talked with him about all that she had on her mind.
1 KINGS 10:2 NIV

According to the writer of 1 Kings, the queen of Sheba visited Solomon in order to test him. The queen's test may well have demanded the best of not only Solomon's wisdom but his diplomatic and political skills as well.

The Bible does not reveal origins or the identity of the queen of Sheba. According to one tradition, she came from Ethiopia. (Ancient Ethiopian lore claimed that Solomon and the queen had a son who grew up to become the African nation's first king.) However, archaeological findings indicate that the Arabian Peninsula is a more likely option. It is also a location that fits well with the biblical narrative.

The ancient peoples of Arabia had accumulated great wealth by importing goods from Asia and Africa and exporting them to their neighbors in the Middle East. Their trade consisted mainly of expensive spices, gold, and precious stones—in other words, the very items the queen presented to Solomon.

Under Solomon, Israel had become a regional power—his kingdom controlled some of the key trade routes that Sheba depended on for its prosperity. In all likelihood, this is what the queen of Sheba "had on her mind" when she tested Solomon's wisdom. Between Solomon's impressive showing—his skills at discernment and negotiation were legendary (see 1 Kings 3:16–28)—and the overwhelming display of his wealth, the queen was awestruck. She honored Israel's king with high praise and a lavish gift of gold, about four and a half tons' worth. Solomon reciprocated by giving the queen "all she desired" (1 Kings 10:13 NIV). The queen of Sheba returned to Arabia, her diplomatic mission a success.

Spiritual Insight:

Jesus taught that the queen of Sheba (to whom he referred as the "Queen of the South" in Matthew 12:42 and Luke 11:31) was more righteous than the religious leaders who opposed Him. When they skeptically demanded proof of His authority, Jesus responded that the queen herself would judge people like them. After all, at least she—though she was a foreigner—had been willing to listen to Solomon's wisdom. Jesus' words are a reminder that religious piety has no value unless it is accompanied by a humble, teachable heart.

Meaning:
--

First Reference:
1 Kings 10:1

Last Reference:
2 Chronicles 9:12

Rahab
RIGHTEOUS PROSTITUTE

*By faith Rahab the prostitute did not perish with those who were
disobedient, because she had given a friendly welcome to the spies.*
HEBREWS 11:31 ESV

You rarely hear the word *righteous* used to describe a prostitute, but that's how the Bible depicts Rahab (James 2:25).
Though God did not condone her occupation, Rahab's faith in
God and her protective actions of the Hebrew spies made her
righteous in God's eyes.

When the Hebrew people were finally ready to take possession of the Promised Land, Joshua sent two spies into Jericho to size up the enemy (Joshua 2). The spies found safe refuge in the home of a prostitute, where it would not have been
unusual for people to be seen coming and going. With such
potential activity, the men found her residence a practical place
to hide and spend the night. While at her home, the spies were
buoyed by the city residents' fear of the Hebrews and by the
help extended to them by Rahab.

In exchange for her protection, the spies gave Rahab instructions that would keep her and her family safe during the upcoming battle. By following these directives, her life was spared when
the city was ravaged. As her final reward, she received an honored place in Israel's history; for, in addition to New Testament
references that laud her faith, some Jewish traditions indicate
that Rahab became the wife of Joshua, the Hebrew leader.

Related Information:

The story of Rahab goes beyond the pages of Joshua and continues into the New Testament Gospels. Tucked in the genealogy of Jesus, we find an unlikely ancestor of the long-awaited Messiah: Rahab. By including unlikely women like Rahab (the prostitute) and Tamar (the woman who had a child with her own father-in-law), God revealed that the Messiah would be the Savior of all people—the likable *and* the undesirables (Matthew 1:5).

Meaning:
Proud

First Reference:
Joshua 2:1

Last Reference:
James 2:25

REBEKAH

ISAAC'S WIFE

Then they said, "Let's call the young woman and ask her about it."
So they called Rebekah and asked her, "Will you go with this man?"
"I will go," she said.
GENESIS 24:57–58 NIV

Pregnancy is not an easy experience—but Rebekah's was so unpleasant that she inquired of the Lord to find out why she was suffering so badly. More amazingly, the Lord answered.

After twenty years of marriage, Rebekah was finally pregnant. It had taken an answer to prayer in order for her and her husband, Isaac, to conceive. The two loved each other—the story of how they came to be married reads like an ancient romance novel. However, without a child, they would be subject to public shame. More important, God's covenant with Rebekah's father-in-law was in jeopardy. How would Abraham become the father of many nations if Isaac and Rebekah could not provide even one offspring?

When Rebekah did become pregnant, however, it was not with just one son but with two. The babies wrestled with one another in the womb, apparently causing Rebekah great discomfort. When she sought an explanation from God, she was told that the sons she bore would give rise to two separate nations. But harmonious coexistence was not what the future held for Rebekah's sons. Puzzlingly, God informed Rebekah that the younger would triumph over the older—precisely the opposite of how it was supposed to be in the ancient Near East.

Things happened exactly as God told Rebekah they would. Of course, Rebekah played a helping hand, favoring her younger son, Jacob, over Esau. Rebekah helped Jacob trick his father into giving him the blessing that was rightfully Esau's. She wanted the best for her younger son, but the best came at a price—estrangement between Jacob and Esau. After Jacob fled on his mother's advice, it is very likely that he never saw Rebekah alive again.

Spiritual Insight:

Rebekah stood in a long line of deceivers. Out of a desire for self-preservation, her father-in-law, Abraham, had tried to convince others that his wife, Sarah, was really just his sister—not once but twice. Rebekah's brother Laban later tricked Jacob into marrying Leah first instead of Rachel. Rebekah prompted Jacob to deceive her own husband. Unfortunately, sinful tendencies have a way of repeating themselves in successive generations. Jacob, for example, came to be regarded as one of the most famous deceivers in the Bible.

Meaning:
Fettering by beauty

First Reference:
Genesis 22:23

Last Reference:
Genesis 49:31

Key References:
Genesis 24:15–25, 62–67; 25:21–26; 27:5–10, 41–46

87

REhoBoam
LAST KING OF A UNITED ISRAEL

*[Rehoboam] followed the advice of the young men and said, "My
father made your yoke heavy; I will make it even heavier. My father
scourged you with whips; I will scourge you with scorpions."*
1 KINGS 12:14 NIV

Despite being the son of one of the wisest men who ever
lived, Rehoboam's bluster proved greater than his compe-
tence to govern.

Rehoboam ascended to the throne immediately upon Solomon's death, but he did not have to wait long to encounter his
first test. Jeroboam, who had fled to Egypt after an unsuccess-
ful rebellion against Solomon, returned to present himself to
Israel's new king. Together with the leaders from the northern
part of the country, Jeroboam made just one request in return
for their loyalty to Rehoboam: they asked him to lighten the
oppressive load that had been placed upon them by Solomon.

In order to consolidate power and make Israel a regional
power, Solomon had levied burdensome taxes—he had even used
forced labor to build God's temple. The people had had enough
and were hoping for a more benevolent ruler in Rehoboam.

How wrong they were.

Instead of listening to seasoned advisers from Solomon's
court, Rehoboam turned to his friends, who seemed to think the
best way for Rehoboam to assert his authority was to be even
more brutish and cruel than his father. So instead of granting the

people's request, Rehoboam promised the opposite.

All but the tribe of Judah abandoned Rehoboam and rallied around Jeroboam. While one of God's prophets managed to dissuade Rehoboam from all-out civil war with the northern tribes, there was conflict between the two kingdoms for the rest of Rehoboam's days.

During his seventeen-year reign, Rehoboam lost territory, wealth, and respect. Worst of all, he set a new low in terms of idolatry—a disheartening standard that would become the benchmark against which Judah's future kings were measured. In addition to erecting pagan places of worship, Rehoboam allowed religious prostitution and actively engaged in the pagan practices of the surrounding nations. Solomon's failure was made complete in his disaster of a son.

Did You Know?

Rehoboam's ironic name borders on the comical. In Hebrew it means "enlarger of the people." Sadly, Rehoboam did the opposite, reducing David and Solomon's kingdom to a fraction of its former glory.

Meaning:
A people has enlarged

First Reference:
1 Kings 11:43

Last Reference:
2 Chronicles 13:7

Key References:
1 Kings 12:1–24; 14:25–28; 2 Chronicles 11:5–14; 12:1–12

Ruth

MOABITE DAUGHTER-IN-LAW OF NAOMI

*But Ruth replied [to Naomi], "Don't urge me to leave you or to turn
back from you. Where you go I will go, and where you stay I will stay.
Your people will be my people and your God my God. Where you
die I will die, and there I will be buried."*
RUTH 1:16–17 NIV

Going the extra mile for someone can be difficult, even
when life is going well. But when there is adversity and
personal turmoil, making an extra effort to help someone else
can seem impossible. In the character of Ruth, however, we see
a shining example of someone doing the impossible.

During the time of the judges in Israel, the family of
Elimelech and Naomi moved to Moab to escape a famine
in Judah. While they were there, one of their sons married a
Moabite woman named Ruth. After ten years of marriage and
the earlier death of her father-in-law, Ruth's husband also died.

Naomi, also widowed, decided to return to Judah with her
husbandless daughters-in-law. On the way, Naomi told them
both to return to their mothers' homes, while she continued
on alone to Judah. One daughter-in-law agreed, but Ruth ada-
mantly refused to leave Naomi. She stayed with her and helped
to provide food for herself and Naomi in Judah by gleaning in
nearby fields—where she eventually met and married Boaz, the
landowner, a relative of Elimelech. Boaz and Ruth later had a
son, Obed, who became the grandfather of King David.

Spiritual Insight:

Even though Ruth may have been suffering tremendous grief over the death of her husband, she didn't return home to the possible comfort of her own family and people. She went with Naomi to a strange land with strange customs, providing comfort and help to her mother-in-law. In our own times of personal distress, would we show others this same selfless kindness? We can rely on God to provide for all our emotional and physical needs—so that we can then demonstrate His love and care to others.

Meaning:
Friend

First Reference:
Ruth 1:4

Last Reference:
Matthew 1:5

Key References:
Ruth 1:14–19; 4:1–10, 13–14

89

Samaritan Woman

WOMAN WHO MET JESUS AT THE WELL

Then, leaving her water jar, the woman went back to the town and said to the people, "Come, see a man who told me everything I ever did. Could this be the Messiah?"
JOHN 4:28–29 NIV

The Samaritan woman must have hated coming to fetch water day after day from the well—all that work, all that gossip about her and her shameful marital situation—but it was at that very well that she found the source of *living* water, which truly satisfies and brings eternal life.

The Samaritans lived in the north-central part of Israel, and they were descended from both Jews and foreign peoples who had been relocated to Israel by the Assyrians hundreds of years earlier. Jews and Samaritans typically despised each other.

When Jesus was traveling from Jerusalem to Galilee, He took the most direct route and passed through Samaria where He met a woman at a well at midday. Jesus spoke to her and offered her living water that brings eternal life, rather than merely water that needed to be fetched day after day from the well. Jesus revealed to the woman that He was aware of her many marital relationships and her current situation of living with a man who was not her husband, and taught her about true worship. She was amazed and went back to her town to tell everyone about Jesus. Many Samaritans turned to Jesus because of the woman's testimony (John 4).

Did You Know?

In the language of Jesus' day, the word for "living" water is the same for "running" water—like a river. The Samaritan was initially interested in Jesus' offer of "living/running" water to avoid having to come to the well each day. Jesus, however, gave her something that truly satisfies the soul.

Meaning:
--

First Reference:
John 4:7

Last Reference:
John 4:39

Samson

Judge and Strongman of Israel

*"No razor shall come upon his head, for the boy shall be
a Nazirite to God from the womb; and he shall begin to
deliver Israel from the hands of the Philistines."*
JUDGES 13:5 NASB

People have married for a host of unusual reasons, but Samson is perhaps one of the few in history to have wedded for the express purpose of picking a fight with the bride's extended family.

Samson was born to Manoah and his wife—a righteous couple who had been barren for years. God revealed that just as Samson's birth was special, so, too, was his life to be special. He was to be set apart, bound by a lifelong Nazirite vow. In the Bible, people were set apart not just for the sake of being different—such honor always had a specific purpose. Samson's purpose was to begin the rebellion against Israel's most notorious oppressors, the Philistines.

As required by the rules governing Nazirite vows, Samson was expected to abstain from three things: alcohol, contact with anything unclean (such as dead bodies), and haircuts.

Before he died, Samson probably violated all three requirements. He behaved as if he were above any rule or responsibility. Even his choice of a wife was baffling to his God-fearing parents, for Samson had demanded to be united to a Philistine woman. This, however, turned out to be one of God's strategic masterstrokes—the writer of 1 Samuel revealed that God used this marriage as an opportunity for Samson to confront the Philistines.

Samson did just that. After Samson decimated their crops, the Philistines murdered Samson's wife and father-in-law. Samson retaliated by going on a violent rampage, nearly bringing the Philistines and their Israelite subjects to full-scale war. In the end, another woman, named Delilah, proved to be Samson's undoing, and Samson's greatest achievement—the destruction of the temple to Dagon and the slaughter of everyone in it—brought about his own death, too.

Spiritual Insight:

Even though the book of Judges portrayed his life as something of a profitable disaster, Samson still managed to earn a mention—albeit a passing one—in the "faith hall of fame" found in the book of Hebrews. Samson's life is an object lesson of both the high cost of sin and God's ability to bring victory from even our greatest failures.

Meaning:
Sunlight

First Reference:
Judges 13:24

Last Reference:
Hebrews 11:32

Key References:
Judges 13:13; 14:4; 16:4–30

Samuel

Prophet and Judge

Samuel continued as Israel's leader all the days of his life.
From year to year he went on a circuit from Bethel to
Gilgal to Mizpah, judging Israel in all those places.
1 Samuel 7:15–16 NIV

Delivering good news does not seem to have been a part of Samuel's job description very often. Yet he was so important to Israel's history that he came to be known as a second Moses (see Jeremiah 15:1).

Like so many others in scripture—Isaac, Samson, and John the Baptist, for example—Samuel was a miracle baby. After pleading with God in the sanctuary at Shiloh, Samuel's mother finally conceived. Hannah had promised that her firstborn son would be devoted to God's service. True to her word, Hannah brought the young boy to Shiloh, where he served under the care of Eli the priest.

Samuel's first encounter with God required him to deliver unsettling news to Eli. God had spoken to Samuel, telling him that his mentor was about to be judged for his failure to restrain his wicked sons, who also served in the sanctuary.

Years later, the Israelites demanded that Samuel appoint a king. God told Samuel to grant the people's request, and then He gave Samuel more bad news to deliver: Israel would come to regret the day they asked for a king. Kings had a way of oppressing their people—seizing their lands and taxing the fruits of their labors. Samuel's prophetic words were fulfilled when Solomon's greed wound up splitting the kingdom in two.

The first choice of king, a man named Saul, proved a disaster, giving Samuel the opportunity to deliver yet another dose of unwelcome news: Saul would not sit long on the throne, and none of his descendants would follow him. Even in death, Samuel delivered bad news for those who disobeyed the Lord. When a desperate King Saul consulted a medium (or witch) at Endor, the figure of Samuel appeared from beyond the grave, telling Saul that he would not live to see another sunset.

Did You Know?

Such was Samuel's reputation that the elders of Bethlehem trembled when the elderly prophet arrived in their town. However, this time Samuel brought good tidings—guided by God, he anointed David to be Saul's replacement.

Meaning:
Heard of God

First Reference:
1 Samuel 1:20

Last Reference:
Hebrews 11:32

Key References:
1 Samuel 1:11, 19–20, 24–28; 3:1–18; 7:3–6, 15–17; 10:1, 20–25; 12:1–25; 15:26; 16:13

92

Sarah

ABRAHAM'S WIFE

By faith even Sarah, who was past childbearing age, was enabled to bear children because she considered him faithful who had made the promise.
HEBREWS 11:11 NIV

Sarah's story is one of belief mixed with doubt. As such, she is a character to which many readers can easily relate.

Most students of the Bible are well acquainted with Sarah's lack of faith. Her skepticism when God promised Abraham a son is understandable—after all, she had more than enough reason to believe this could never happen. Sarah had aged well beyond childbearing years when God spoke to her husband for the first time. Also, Sarah and Abraham were nearly parted from each other on at least two occasions—both times thanks to Abraham's own apparent lack of faith. In strikingly similar episodes, two rulers—first the king of Egypt, then the king of Gerar—took Sarah to be their wife. To save his own skin, Abraham had passed off Sarah as his sister (which was half true, since, in addition to being husband and wife, Sarah and Abraham were half siblings).

However, God's plan for Sarah would not be thwarted—not by outside events and not even by Sarah's own actions. Having long since given up on the hope of bearing a son, Sarah gave her servant Hagar to Abraham, in accordance with an ancient Mesopotamian custom. This union had the desired effect: Hagar gave birth to Ishmael. But things soured when Sarah turned on Hagar.

Despite her many doubts, however, Sarah was not entirely without faith. After all, she stood by Abraham during the entire twenty-five years that transpired between the first promise and its eventual fulfillment in the birth of Isaac. She may have laughed at the thought of a son, but she did not entirely abandon hope. In fact, the prophet Isaiah held up Sarah as a model of trust in God's faithfulness, counseling the people to "look to Abraham, your father, and to Sarah, who gave you birth" (Isaiah 51:2 NIV).

Did You Know?

As further evidence of Sarah's faith, it is possible to translate Hebrews 11:11 as a statement about her: "By faith even Sarah, who was past age, was enabled to bear children because she considered him faithful who had made the promise" (see NIV footnote to Hebrews 11:11).

Meaning:
Female noble

First Reference:
Genesis 17:15

Last Reference:
Romans 9:9

Key References:
Genesis 18:10–15; 21:1–10; 23:1–20

93

Saul

Israel's First King

*"To obey is better than sacrifice, and to heed is better than
the fat of rams. . . . Because you have rejected the word
of the Lord, he has rejected you as king."*
1 Samuel 15:22–23 niv

As far as disasters go, Saul's time on the throne was an unmitigated one. At first, the man with the impressive physique tried to resist his appointment as king of Israel. He did not consider himself suited to the job. He was, as he reminded Samuel, a member of "the smallest tribe of Israel"; his clan was "the least of all the clans of the tribe of Benjamin" (1 Samuel 9:21 niv). Apparently, many of Saul's own subjects were inclined to agree. After his first coronation, some openly questioned whether Saul was up to the job of delivering Israel.

Soon, however, Saul won over the doubters when he rallied a massive army to come to the aid of Jabesh Gilead, just east of the Jordan River. The victory prompted a second coronation ceremony—this one marked by the people's enthusiastic celebration of their new king.

Unfortunately, Saul's triumph was short-lived. For the rest of his reign, he proved erratic and unstable. More than once he failed to listen to the prophet Samuel—as a result, Samuel announced that the throne would be taken from Saul. When God chose David as Saul's successor, the king of Israel became even more dangerously paranoid. Though David would not lift a finger against him, Saul made repeated attempts on the young warrior's life. So obsessed was Saul that he slaughtered eighty-five priests suspected of aiding David and even began neglecting his royal duties. While Saul schemed, it was left to David to deliver the town of Keilah from the Philistines—the very enemy whom Saul had been raised up to fight.

Saul's life ended in humiliating defeat to the Philistines. His failure was complete, and the nation of Israel was in disarray.

Spiritual Insight:

Despite being enemies, David never completely lost his regard for Saul. Such was David's honor that on the first occasion when he spared Saul's life, he was "conscience-stricken" over merely cutting a corner of his robe (see 1 Samuel 24:5 NIV). When Saul was finally killed, David responded with a touching lament for Israel's fallen king (2 Samuel 1:19–27). Long before Jesus came, David demonstrated what it looks like to "love your enemies" (see Matthew 5:44 NIV).

Meaning:
Asked

First Reference:
1 Samuel 9:2

Last Reference:
Acts 13:21

Key References:
1 Samuel 10:1, 17–24; 13:8–14; 15:1–3, 8–14, 35;
18:1–2, 5–11; 28:7–19; 31:1–4

94

Silas

Leader of the Early Church

*About midnight Paul and Silas were praying and singing hymns to God,
and the other prisoners were listening to them. Suddenly there was such a
violent earthquake that the foundations of the prison were shaken.*
Acts 16:25–26 NIV

Silas was a gifted leader and a fearless adventurer. In addition, he may have aided in the composition of at least one New Testament book.

As a leader in the Jerusalem church, Silas was among those chosen to deliver the congregation's letter to Gentile believers in Antioch, Syria, and Cilicia. Silas lent credibility to the expedition, which also included Paul, Barnabas, and Judas Barsabbas. Silas, however, was far more than a letter carrier—in Antioch, he further encouraged the believers by prophesying to them. The content of Silas's teaching is not revealed in the book of Acts, but the result was that all the Gentile Christians were greatly encouraged.

Later, when Paul and Barnabas parted ways over their disagreement concerning Mark (see Acts 15:36–41), Paul invited Silas to accompany him to Syria and Cilicia. Their plans changed abruptly, however, when Paul received a vision of a man begging them to come to Macedonia. With that, the pair introduced the gospel to the area that is present-day Greece. They were even imprisoned during their stay in Philippi. After a massive earthquake, however, their jailer (who was amazed to discover that Silas and Paul had not seized their opportunity to flee) converted to Christianity and invited them to his house. After that, the two were released.

Silas made an ideal traveling companion for Paul. Both were Roman citizens (see Acts 16:37), a fact that proved useful for getting out of difficult situations like the one at Philippi. Silas may have also had a way with words. Both letters to the church at Thessalonica were said to be from "Paul, Silas, and Timothy" (see 1 Thessalonians 1:1; 2 Thessalonians 1:1). Years later, the apostle Peter credited Silas with helping him write his first letter (see 1 Peter 5:12). Although he did not play a leading role himself, Silas proved a vital partner to two of the early church's greatest apostles.

Did You Know?
In three New Testament books (2 Corinthians, 1 Thessalonians, and 1 Peter) Silas is referred to as "Silvanus." Apparently "Silas" was a contraction of his full name.

Meaning:
Sylvan

First Reference:
Acts 15:22

Last Reference:
1 Peter 5:12

Key References:
Acts 15:38–41; 16:16–40

Solomon
King of Israel

*"So give your servant a discerning heart to govern your
people and to distinguish between right and wrong.
For who is able to govern this great people of yours?"*
1 Kings 3:9 niv

Solomon had everything going for him: wisdom, wealth, and
power. Unfortunately, he had many vices as well: greed, lust,
and idolatry. These combined to bring about the undoing of
Israel in more ways than one.

Solomon was not the obvious choice for the throne. Nevertheless, David handpicked Solomon as his successor. While
Solomon eventually took his place as one of the few truly great
kings of Israel, he was very different from his father. David was
a warrior, accustomed to dealing with conflict (or at least the
threat of conflict) for most of his rule. By contrast, Solomon
presided over the most enduring peace in Israel's history.

Without pressures from beyond his kingdom, Solomon
devoted himself to other pursuits—namely, cultivating wisdom
(which he famously displayed to the amazement of his subjects
and foreign dignitaries alike), forging diplomatic alliances with
regional powers like Egypt, and building the temple in Jerusalem.

Solomon, however, was not without his blind spots. His
wisdom (a gift from God, according to the writer of 1 Kings)
did not prevent him from plunging headlong into the dangerous pursuit of wealth. He accumulated chariots and horses in

violation of God's command (see Deuteronomy 17:16). He used forced labor to build the temple and taxed the people heavily in order to finance his luxurious lifestyle (see 1 Kings 5:13; 12:4). Solomon's best-known weakness, however, was his taste for women—and lots of them. Solomon famously had seven hundred wives—many of them no doubt marriages arranged for diplomatic reasons—and another three hundred concubines. Like the practice of accumulating wealth, the king's taking of many wives was expressly forbidden by the Law (see Deuteronomy 17:17), and for good reason. Over time, Solomon's pagan wives lured him away from the one true God. And as the story ends, the once wise king descends into folly.

Spiritual Insight:

When he dedicated the temple, Solomon expressed a profound truth about God: no building can contain His presence (see 2 Chronicles 6:18–21). God in His grace condescends to move among us, but His presence and power cannot be confined to any building or box.

Meaning:
Peaceful

First Reference:
2 Samuel 5:14

Last Reference:
Acts 7:47

Key References:
2 Samuel 12:24; 1 Kings 3:1–14; 5:1–6;
6:1; 8:22–61; 10:1–3; 11:1–8, 11–13

STEPHEN

FIRST CHRISTIAN MARTYR

*But Stephen, full of the Holy Spirit, looked up to heaven and saw the
glory of God, and Jesus standing at the right hand of God.*
ACTS 7:55 NIV

Stephen's death marked a crucial turning point for the
church. Not only was it the beginning of the first great
persecution of believers, but it set the stage for Saul—one of
the great enemies of the church—to become one of its most
important figures.

Stephen was a Hellenistic (Greek) Jew who embraced Jesus as his Messiah and quickly rose to prominence among the
believers. He was renowned for his faith and became the first
person outside the apostles to perform miracles in the name
of Jesus. So Stephen was an obvious choice when the fledgling
church needed to appoint godly individuals to oversee the care
of its most vulnerable members: its widows. Unique among
the seven men who were appointed, Stephen does not seem
to have been confined to this task. He also ministered among
the people, proclaiming Christ in public view. This, combined
with his knack for debating his opponents into stunned silence,
made him an easy target. Soon enough, Stephen was seized
and dragged before the Sanhedrin, the Jewish ruling council.

Stephen laid the blame for Jesus' death on the Sanhedrin. At
that point, they took him outside the city gates and stoned him
to death. Before dying, Stephen caught a glimpse of Jesus—his

advocate and his justifier—standing at God's right hand.

Stephen's martyrdom set off persecution of the church in Jerusalem—but it was precisely this persecution that scattered the disciples and helped spread the gospel throughout Judea and Samaria.

Spiritual Insight:

With his final breath, Stephen cried out a prayer reminiscent of the words Jesus spoke from the cross: "Lord, do not hold this sin against them" (Acts 7:60 NIV). Indeed, God showed His mercy to one of the conspirators behind the murder of Stephen and the ensuing persecution of the church. Saul (later named Paul) was instrumental in both. Not even one of the greatest enemies of the church was beyond the kind of forgiveness that Stephen prayed for.

Meaning:
Wreathe

First Reference:
Acts 6:5

Last Reference:
Acts 22:20

Syrophoenician Woman

MOTHER OF A DEMON-POSSESSED DAUGHTER

Then Jesus said to her, "Woman, you have great faith!
Your request is granted." And her daughter was healed at that moment.
MATTHEW 15:28 NIV

The story of the encounter between Jesus and the unnamed Syrophoenician woman has puzzled many readers. Why did Jesus appear eager to brush off the woman at first? Why did He seem to think her ethnicity was a valid reason to refuse her request—especially since it concerned the well-being of her little girl? Most of all, why did Jesus change His mind? Had He been mistaken and, realizing the error of His thinking, decided to grant the woman's request after all? Or was it all a setup designed to test the woman's persistence?

It is unlikely, to say the least, that Jesus viewed the Syrophoenician woman disdainfully on account of her ethnicity. After all, Jesus had nearly gotten Himself killed at the synagogue in His hometown for reminding His fellow Jews of a time when God sent the prophets not to His chosen people but to people like Naaman the Syrian (see Luke 4:24–27). At the end of His earthly ministry, Jesus commissioned His disciples to take the gospel to "all nations" (see Matthew 28:19 NIV).

Scholars note that Jesus' explanation—"It is not right to

take the children's bread and toss it to the dogs" (Matthew 15:26 NIV)—was not a rejection of this woman and her fellow Gentiles but a statement about the focus of Jesus' immediate ministry. He had been sent to His fellow Jews—and while this did not preclude Him from ministering among the Gentiles, His immediate focus remained on His own people.

Some suggest that Jesus may have used His exchange with the Syrophoenician woman as a test of her faith—or perhaps as a teachable moment with His disciples. Matthew noted that it was the disciples who had pressed Jesus to send the woman away. In the end, the woman triumphed—her faith and persistence mattered more than her ethnicity. Impressed by her tenacity, Jesus healed the woman's demon-possessed daughter.

Spiritual Insight:

The Syrophoenician woman's response to Jesus' initial rebuff demonstrated not only her persistence but her quick thinking, too. Playing off Jesus' own metaphor of children and their dogs (the Greek word most likely refers to a puppy taken as a pet), the woman responded that she would accept whatever Jesus had to offer. Such unconditional acceptance was what won Jesus' admiration and respect.

Meaning:
--

First Reference:
Matthew 15:22

Last Reference:
Mark 7:30

98

Thomas

DOUBTING APOSTLE

Then Jesus told him, "Because you have seen me, you have believed;
blessed are those who have not seen and yet have believed."
JOHN 20:29 NIV

Thomas is best known for his doubting tendencies, but the disciple of Jesus also known as Didymus was capable of demonstrating courage and resolve, too.

When his friend Lazarus died, Jesus set out for Bethany, near Jerusalem—not to pay His last respects, but to raise Lazarus from the dead. However, doing so meant walking straight into His enemies' lair. The disciples were aware of the dangers. Jesus had already alluded to His death (see John 10:15), and of course they were not blind to opposition of the religious leaders. They knew going to Bethany was risky. Yet Thomas alone spoke in favor of Jesus' plan, saying that if their Master was going to die, the rest of them may as well die with Him.

This episode of courage is overshadowed by Thomas's infamous display of doubt following the resurrection of Jesus. Thomas had been away when Jesus first appeared to the disciples. Upon hearing the news, he refused to believe it—until Jesus appeared yet again, astonishing the skeptical disciple.

It is easy to judge Thomas harshly. However, to do so is to forget that bodily resurrections were not exactly an everyday occurrence in the first century. Even the fact that Thomas had seen his Master raise others from the dead could have been forgotten easily in the grief and confusion that followed Jesus' crucifixion.

Thomas was not condemned by Jesus, nor was his belief rejected. Nevertheless, the risen Lord used the occasion to bless those who would believe in Him even without seeing.

Did You Know?

There are competing accounts of Thomas's life following the resurrection of Jesus. According to one tradition, he ventured as far as India. However, the early church theologian Origen wrote that Thomas brought the gospel to Parthia, which included parts of present-day Turkey, Iraq, and Iran. He is said to have died in Edessa, present-day Turkey. Whatever his contribution to the spread of Christianity may have been, Thomas was almost certainly a part of it. After all, he was present with the other disciples after Jesus ascended to heaven (see Acts 1:13).

Meaning:
The twin

First Reference:
Matthew 10:3

Last Reference:
Acts 1:13

Key References:
John 11:16; 20:24–29

99

Timothy

DISCIPLE OF PAUL

To Timothy my true son in the faith: Grace, mercy and
peace from God the Father and Christ Jesus our Lord.
1 TIMOTHY 1:2 NIV

The uncircumcised son of a Jewish mother and a Gentile father, Timothy was the last person one would have expected
Paul—a former Pharisee—to choose as his disciple.

The fact that Timothy was the product of a mixed marriage
would have been enough cause for a scandal among his fellow
Jews. It was probably Timothy's father who kept him from
being circumcised as a baby—Gentiles in the Greco-Roman
world considered it a mutilation of the male human figure,
which was revered as one of the highest forms of beauty. In any
case, Timothy's uncircumcised state is a strong indicator that
his father was not just a Gentile, but a pagan as well.

Without the mark of the circumcision, Timothy probably was not fully welcomed by the Jewish community in his
hometown of Lystra, in present-day Turkey. He may have been
labeled a *mamzer*—regarded as an illegitimate child in the eyes
of his fellow Jews. Nevertheless, Timothy devoted himself to
the Old Testament scriptures, aided by his devout mother and
grandmother, Lois.

When Paul—who had once believed that circumcision
and the law were all that mattered—arrived in Lystra, Timothy caught his attention. Hearing nothing but praise from the
Christians already present there, Paul decided that Timothy

should accompany him on his journey. In order not to cause unnecessary offense among the local Jews, Paul had Timothy circumcised—apparently this is the kind of thing that becoming "all things to all men" (1 Corinthians 9:22 NASB) involved. Perhaps more than anything else, the fact that Timothy was willing to undergo such a painful procedure as an adult indicates the depth of his devotion to Christ and His church.

Timothy went on to become the pastor of the church at Ephesus, approximately 250–300 miles west of his hometown. The assignment brought its share of challenges, but Timothy had the writings of his mentor, Paul, to encourage him along the way.

Spiritual Insight:

Timothy is a well-known reminder that age is not a barrier to serving God's kingdom. Paul famously encouraged Timothy, who was by this time assigned to the church at Ephesus, not to "let anyone look down" (1 Timothy 4:12 NIV) on him because of his youth. Anyone—no matter how young—can set an example for all God's people.

Meaning:
Dear to God

First Reference:
2 Corinthians 1:1

Last Reference:
Hebrews 13:23

Key References:
1 Timothy 1:2; 6:20–21

100

WOMAN CAUGHT IN ADULTERY

UNNAMED WOMAN SPARED BY JESUS

Jesus straightened up and asked her, "Woman, where are they? Has no one condemned you?" "No one, sir," she said. "Then neither do I condemn you," Jesus declared. "Go now and leave your life of sin."
JOHN 8:10–11 NIV

When the Jewish religious leaders dragged the adulterous woman before Jesus, He did not question her guilt. However, the entire situation reeked of injustice—which Jesus masterfully exposed in His response.

The adulterous woman provided the bait in the Pharisees' trap. Aside from this, nothing is known about her—or how the religious leaders managed to catch her "in the act" of committing adultery. They pretended to be concerned with fidelity to the law of Moses, yet nothing could have been further from the truth. Otherwise, they would have apprehended the guilty man as well, since the Law held *both* parties accountable in cases of adultery (see Leviticus 20:10).

The religious leaders intended to use the woman's plight to trap Jesus in a no-win situation. If He disagreed with the suggestion that she be stoned, He would be accused of going against the Torah—the very Law He had come to "fulfill" (see Matthew 5:17). But if Jesus agreed with their sentence, He would be challenging the power of Rome, which had the exclusive authority to mete out capital punishment.

Perhaps the woman held her breath as Jesus invited the religious leaders to stone her—provided they were without sin themselves, that is. According to Jesus, only a righteous judge would do—and the only truly righteous judge in their midst (the Lord Himself) chose not to throw any stones. Instead, having silenced His opponents, Jesus sent the woman on her way, with the loving admonition to leave behind the destructive life that had gotten her into this mess in the first place.

Did You Know?

The earliest manuscripts of John do not contain this story of the woman caught in adultery. As further evidence that it was not original to John's Gospel, some experts note that the first verse (John 7:53) does not fit the preceding context. However, the story is consistent with the overall life and teachings of Jesus, leading a number of scholars to conclude that it is nonetheless authentic—just misplaced somehow. (There's even one family of manuscripts that puts the story at the end of Luke 21.)

Meaning:
--

First Reference:
John 8:3

Last Reference:
John 8:11

ZEChARiah

FATHER OF JOHN THE BAPTIST

Zechariah asked the angel, "How can I be sure of this?
I am an old man and my wife is well along in years."
LUKE 1:18 NIV

Though he may have had a rather common name (there are no fewer than twelve Zechariahs mentioned in the Bible), this particular Zechariah stood out as father to the forerunner of the Messiah.

Zechariah and his wife, Elizabeth, echoed a recurring theme from the Jewish story: barrenness and the accompanying sense of emptiness. In their world, bearing children meant the all-important survival of the family line. Being unable to conceive was taken as the absence of God's blessing.

However, Zechariah had been blessed in other ways, and there was no question of his integrity. A member of the Levite priestly class, he belonged to one of twenty-four divisions (his was the division of Abijah) that took turns serving in the temple at Jerusalem. According to the Gospel writer Luke, both he and his wife were blameless in God's sight. Luke wanted to make sure his readers understood that their barren situation was in no way the result of some undisclosed sin.

One day during his service, Zechariah was chosen to burn incense before the Most Holy Place inside the temple. Given the number of priests available for service, it was not an honor that one received very often. For Zechariah, an already unforgettable experience was made even more unusual by the appearance of an angel who announced the impossible: Zechariah and Elizabeth would bear a son. Their son would be subject to a lifetime Nazirite vow, much like Samson, and he would be counted as the greatest of the old prophets (see Matthew 11:7–13).

Zechariah seemed to believe it was too good to be true, despite knowing the stories of Sarah, Rebekah, Rachel, and Hannah. In response to his demand for a sign, the angel gave him one: He would be mute until the child was born. Having gotten the message but being unable to share it with others (see Luke 1:22), Zechariah returned home. Everything happened just as the angel said it would.

Did You Know?

Zechariah appeared once more in the story, overruling the custom of naming the firstborn after the father in order to obey the angel's instructions. The story reveals that the naming of the child, which took place at his circumcision on the eighth day, was apparently a community affair.

Meaning:
God has remembered

First Reference:
Luke 1:5

Last Reference:
Luke 3:2

SCRIPTURE INDEX